Handbook of
Strategic Growth
Through
Mergers and Acquisitions

WILLIAM K. SMITH

Touche Ross & Co.

Prentice-Hall, Inc.
Englewood Cliffs, New Jersey

Editora Prentice-Hall do Brasil Ltda., *Rio de Janeiro*
Prentice-Hall International, Inc., *London*
Prentice-Hall of Australia, Pty. Ltd., *Sydney*
Prentice-Hall Canada Inc., *Toronto*
Prentice-Hall of India Private Ltd., *New Delhi*
Prentice-Hall of Japan, Inc., *Tokyo*
Prentice-Hall of Southeast Asia Pte. Ltd., *Singapore*
Whitehall Books, Ltd., *Wellington, New Zealand*
Prentice-Hall Hispanoamericana, S.A., *Mexico*

This publication is designed to provide accurate and authoritative information in regard
to the subject matter covered. It is sold with the understanding that by this product
neither the publisher nor the author is engaged in rendering legal, accounting, or other
professional services. If professional advice is required, the services of a competent
professional person should be sought.

Library of Congress Cataloging in Publication Data

Smith, William K. (William Kevin)
  Handbook of strategic growth through mergers and
acquisitions.

  Includes index.
  1. Consolidation and merger of corporations—Handbooks,
manuals, etc. I. Title.
HD2746.5.S65 1985   658.1′6   84–22273

ISBN 0-13-381815-2

Printed in the United States of America

Preface

A merger or an acquisition is the most dramatic route a company can take in the implementation of its strategic plan. Overnight, a company can become a major force in a new market or have a new distribution network for its products and services. The impact of a merger or an acquisition can be as dramatic in its success as it can be in its failure. The purpose of this book is to assist corporations in successfully achieving their corporate goals through merger or acquisition by applying proven strategic planning and corporate finance techniques to the process.

History has shown that many corporations are not prepared to undertake an acquisition. Devising an effective growth planning process can take many months and demands commitment from the highest levels of management. Implementing a strategic growth plan with a merger or an acquisition combines the disciplines of corporate finance, strategic planning, corporate taxation, accounting, operations, marketing and human resources.

The *Handbook of Strategic Growth Through Mergers and Acquisitions* is designed to cover the complete merger and acquisition process. This work starts with developing the strategic growth plan; goes on to describe the process of finding, analyzing, valuing, and negotiating with candidates; and finally ends with detailing guidelines on how to successfully integrate the new company.

The book was written from the perspective of a corporate acquiror, but it should prove equally useful to companies interested in selling themselves or divesting a division. The topics which the book addresses are of concern to the chief executive officer making the merger or acquisition decision, corporate development officers, division managers, corporate advisors, and executives responsible for implementing the strategic growth plan.

ACKNOWLEDGMENTS

This book brings together many technical disciplines related to the subject of mergers and acquisitions. In this regard the author expresses his gratitude to the corporate finance, tax, accounting and management consulting professionals who make up the Touche Ross Financial Services Center. They have lent their business expertise to make this book one that is practical and technically sound. Concepts contained within this book are drawn from actual assignments undertaken in the merger and acquisition field.

I would like to thank Mr. R. B. Hoover, Partner and Director of the Touche Ross Corporate Finance Group, for challenging many of the thoughts expressed here. A special thanks goes to Mr. J. Thomas Presby, Partner in Charge of the Financial Services Center, for his advice, counsel, and support of this endeavor. I owe an intellectual debt to several outstanding Touche Ross Financial Services Center partners who have assisted in molding many of the concepts contained in this book, including: Kenneth F. Cooper, an expert in the area of banking and finance; James P. Duffy, a corporate finance partner with broad industry exposure in operations and finance; Richard A. Patterson, also in corporate finance with over 10 years of private industry experience in strategic planning and mergers and acquisitions; Robert S. Kay, James A. Johnson, and Robert N. Waxman, specialist in consulting to the investment banking community on tax, accounting and regulatory issues concerning business combinations.

For their encouragement, support, and advice, I would like to thank Mr. Edward A. Kangas and Mr. John E. Temple, two prominent management consultants for whom I hold a great deal of respect. Edwin H. Ruzinsky, Ronald P. Brotherton and Robert Bartels, partners from Touche Ross's Executive Office, were extremely helpful in the publishing of this document.

Finally, I am indebted to Fuad Saba for his help in tightening up the manuscript and making this work eminently more readable than it otherwise might have been.

William K. Smith

To Kathleen Shelton Smith

Contents

Introduction

1

EXECUTIVES, investment bankers, attorneys, accountants, and consultants have long sought the key to successful acquisitions or mergers—some unfailing talisman that might guide them to success and ward off unrewarding liaisons. Until such a magical device is discovered, a structured program and hard work are your best hope for a successful deal.

For some, a deal is concluded once the ink is dry and fees have been collected. However, as many executives have learned, this is really when the hardest work begins and the point at which the true success of the merger or acquisition is either established or destroyed. Like its human counterpart, the corporate "divorce" (divestiture) rate has ballooned over the last decade—some place it at 70 percent. Keep in mind that there have been more than 60,000 mergers in the United States. And many companies brought together by merger or acquisition are now in evident disharmony.

The central thread running through this book is the relationship between buyer and the acquired company. A few years ago, Professor Rumelt of UCLA published a study of acquisitions made by the 500 largest industrial companies over a period of 25 years. He found that the most successful results were obtained when buyers acquired in fields close to their own; conversely, the poorest results were obtained when buyers diversified into areas unrelated to their own.

Clearly then, the fit between buyer and target is critical to the success of an acquisition or merger. We will talk a great deal in this book about how to study candidates, what to look for, and how to negotiate a sale. But all of it will have one goal in mind: to ensure, as far as possible, that the combined entity that results from the merger or acquisition will be as healthy as possible. The goal is to form a combined company that capitalizes on the strengths of its parts, always looking for synergies and helping to overcome each part's weak points. Our strategy is to optimize the fit between the two companies involved and not necessarily trying to get the best deal. Buying a suit on sale is not a good deal if it's not your size.

So we begin by studying the buyer's company (Chapter 2). Only when you have a clear perception of your own position can you usefully evaluate the fit between yours and a candidate company you are considering. Then you search for and screen candidates (Chapter 3), based on criteria related to your own company's profile. When you have narrowed the field of candidates, it's time to dig in and learn everything you can (Chapter 4), so you'll have a sound basis for negotiating with the seller (Chaper 5). Chapter 6 deals with setting the price, and Chapter 7 offers advice on the critically important process of integrating the two companies.

Obviously this is a highly structured method. And you may well ask if the full procedure is really necessary. After all, if you happen onto a spectacular bargain, why not jump at the opportunity? A real bargain might slip away to another buyer while I'm busy going through all this analysis. Isn't an experienced manager's intuition worth something?

As you'll discover, this book attempts to take the guesswork, but not the intuition, out of mergers and acquisitions. But, in following this method, your intuition will fall into a framework created by your hard work, painstaking analysis, and vigilance.

If you're thinking that all the analysis is unnecessary, that you should simply watch for a bargain and jump when it comes along, we offer you two thoughts. One, careful analysis beforehand of your own company will put you in a much better position to know which bargains are truly bargains for you. Two, probably no more than half of all corporate mergers and acquisitions succeed over the long term. For example, Rockwell's 1980 acquisition of Wescom was hailed by Rockwell executives as a show of bidding genius. And, to be fair, it may have been well negotiated. But Rockwell's failure to turn Wescom around merely served to sap its own strength (and caused it a great deal of embarrassment). And in 1981, the bidding war between DuPont, Mobil, and Seagram for control of Conoco cost DuPont, the "winner," a 100 percent premium, or about $7.5 billion. These are only two examples of what can happen and what might be avoided by more careful study and planning and a better underlying strategy. The fact that over 2,500 acquisitions were reported in 1983 alone accounts for the large number of corporate "divorces" likely to take place before long. The structured method described in this book can help avoid such misfortune.

Why do buyers buy? There are risks associated with mergers and acquisitions, to be sure, but there can be substantial rewards as well. In a survey of corporate directors, Touche Ross & Co., the international accounting, tax and management consulting firm, has discovered that these rewards may include an expanded or better-rounded product line, cost savings owing to combined marketing and distribution, a strengthened management team, immediate access to cash or debt capacity, integration (forward, back, or horizontal), and tax benefits. We will say more in later chapters about these benefits.

While this book is primarily intended for buyers, we will encourage you again and again to look at the deal from the seller's point of view, to understand his or her situation and motivations. Why do sellers sell?

Some corporations divest themselves of subsidiaries when a past merger or acquisition has failed to achieve anticipated results. Sometimes a corporate slimming down helps to boost the performance of its stock. The following is a partial list of reasons why sellers sell.

1. Company decides to focus its resources into new markets and sell off subsidiaries not consistent with its new strategy
2. Company is not able to manage successfully its subsidiary
3. Company needs capital to support the growth of other areas of the company
4. Owners want to retire
5. Depressed market in the company's area
6. Competition squeezing this company out
7. Expensive union settlements coming up
8. Supply problems
9. Franchise cancellation
10. Threat of major lawsuits

You'll uncover the last few items during your analysis of candidate companies. This study can help avoid painful surprises. But first, analyze your own situation and develop a growth plan—which is the subject of Chapter 2.

Developing a
Growth Plan

2

ACQUISITIONS reflect management's intended direction for a company. They can open up new growth opportunities and close off others. Through acquisition a company can quickly enter new markets, gain new technologies, and obtain new talents. In short, an acquisition is a dramatic avenue to corporate growth.

Managers can reduce their risks in acquisitions, and generally in making growth decisions, by developing a plan for corporate growth. Such a plan is a blueprint for allocating limited resources to ensure continued growth and profitability. Growth planning entails continually analyzing existing and potential markets, products, and competitors, and systematically applying corporate resources. Strategic decisions are then translated into current as well as long-term operations.

The development of a growth plan consists of five steps:

- Developing a corporate profile
- Establishing a corporate mission
- Setting goals for growth
- Developing an industry profile
- Choosing alternatives for action

In the case of an acquisition, this general model should also include criteria for choosing candidates (as covered in Chapter 4).

Most companies do not develop thorough growth plans. Instead

11

of setting goals and then analyzing only those candidates consistent with their goals, they waste time analyzing companies that—they discover too late—do not support their growth strategy. Without a growth plan, analyzing candidates is often a waste of managers' time. Acquiring a company and later divesting it because "it doesn't fit" can be a financial disaster.

Managers may change their growth plan to rationalize an acquisition. This is particularly true of acquirers who take over a company without taking time to find out whether the candidate fits into their own growth plans. Managers may justify such actions by saying that they are taking advantage of a great opportunity that will be lost unless they act quickly.

Acting quickly and changing plans may take advantage of apparent opportunities, but it certainly does not lead to consistent growth. Corporations experienced in takeovers plan for opportunities. Such firms constantly study industries and specific companies. When an opportunity to acquire arises, they act quickly and reduce their risk because they've already studied the company they are buying.

2.1 FORMING THE ACQUISITION TEAM

The acquisition team is most often headed by the corporate development department, which in turn reports directly to the CEO and/or chairman of the board. Other important participants may be drawn from the Board of Directors, or might include division heads, members of the legal department, or outside acquisition professionals. In smaller organizations, the entire acquisition team might consist of only the CEO or proprietor.

Although the corporate development department may coordinate the acquisition effort, the CEO and the Board usually make the final decision to acquire. The activities of the corporate development department are centered upon information gathering and analysis. The department coordinates the work of corporate managers and outside consultants throughout the acquisition process. It monitors progress and reports all major developments to the CEO. In effect, it synthesizes analyses and judgments for presentation to the decision makers.

More specifically, the corporate development department typically includes the following acquisition responsibilities:

- Establish and maintain relationships with key organizations that can help provide leads to acquisition candidates (bankers, accountants, acquisition consultants, finders, and so forth)
- Maintain an acquisition target log
- Conduct screening studies and market research
- Prepare acquisition studies
- Participate in negotiations
- Conduct due diligence of acquisition targets
- Prepare special investment studies
- Serve as liaison between senior corporate management and other members of the acquisition team

The corporate development team must have a long-term view of the direction of the firm. They should see how well the proposed acquisition will fit their company's strategic goals, and they should assess their company's ability to successfully integrate the new acquisition (see Chapter 7).

The corporate development department typically works with several other departments and/or individuals within the acquiring organization. These other individuals provide functional expertise or industry knowledge to the acquisition team. It is important to recognize that different groups within an organization are likely to have different views toward a particular acquisition. It is the responsibility of the corporate development department to ensure that the ultimate decision to acquire or not to acquire will be based strictly on the organization's strategic needs and on objective analytical evidence. Accordingly, they will have to balance managerial insights and impressions with formal documentation to justify the acquisition.

Outside acquisition professionals often provide valuable assistance in the merger and acquisition process. Drawing on their past experience in similar transactions, outside professionals can act as confidential advisors to the company.

The valuation opinion is one important service usually provided to companies by outside professionals. This objective analysis combines several technical disciplines. It can help a company avoid paying too much for a candidate. Conversely, an outside valuation opinion can help assess the proper selling price for a divestiture.

An outside professional can act as an advocate for the company throughout the negotiations. Additionally, a professional should be able to provide financial structuring and tax advice to successfully conclude

Figure 2–1 Professional Merger and Acquisition Services

1. *Services to Potential Acquirers*
   - Planning phase
     —review and development of acquisition plans
     —establishment of target company criteria
     —industry analyses
     —candidate company identification
     —candidate screening
     —candidate approach
   - Execution phase
     —acquisition analysis
       - financial justification
       - return on investment
       - sensitivity analyses
     —acquisition structuring
       - transaction terms planning
       - negotiation assistance
       - tax advice
       - accounting advice
     —valuation/fairness opinions
     —business review
     —acquisition audit
     —closing assistance
   - Post-transaction phase
     —integration planning
     —systems interfacing
     —operations rationalization
     —deployment of human resources
     —organization structuring
     —accounting and financial integration

14

2. *Services to Potential Sellers*

- Planning phase

  —cash out/divestment alternative evaluation

  —acquirer criteria development

  —offering memorandum preparation

  —valuation/fairness opinion

  —buyer identification

  —pricing strategy development

- Execution phase

  —transaction structuring

  - transaction terms planning

  - negotiation assistance

  - tax advice

  - accounting advice

  —closing assistance

- Post-transaction phase

  —reinvestment strategy review and development

  —balance sheet structuring

the transaction. Figure 2–1 shows the services offered to potential acquirers and sellers by outside professional merger and acquisition advisors.

2.2   DEVELOPING A CORPORATE PROFILE

A corporate profile shows where your company is today. It helps establish formal goals and identify strategies the company can undertake. The profile:

1. Analyzes the threats, opportunities, strengths, and weaknesses your company faces
2. Assesses your company's ability to undertake acquisitions

ANALYZING THREATS, OPPORTUNITIES, STRENGTHS, AND WEAKNESSES

One reason to develop a growth plan is to assess threats and opportunities so that you may act today to make the best of both.

Before studying a prospect, you should understand the opportunities and threats facing your company. You then can judge whether an acquisition will move your company closer to or further from a threat or opportunity. Identifying opportunities is one of the most valuable parts of good planning. You also should consider the possibility and cost of eliminating major threats, particularly those that your competitors have been unable to solve.

Opportunities and threats are potential external events that do not yet affect your company, but might do so in the future. Using a simple example, suppose you learn that retail customers show a high preference for your company's products, even though your company's distribution to the retail channel is limited. You have an opportunity to increase your sales if you can increase your distribution to retailers. Conversely, you have found a threat when you discover that a competitor plans to introduce a new product aimed at gaining greater market share.

When evaluating such events, it is useful to quantify by estimating probabilities and potential effects on earnings. To weigh opportunities and threats, you may construct an Opportunity/Threat Matrix, as shown in Figure 2–2.

The matrix in Figure 2–2 is constructed by applying management's judgment to selected future events. These events are characterized either as opportunities (if the event is expected to have a positive effect on company earnings), or as threats (if the outcome adversely affects company earnings). Opportunities are placed above the zero mark indicated along the vertical axis, and threats are placed below that mark.

Figure 2-2. Hypothetical Opportunity/Threat Matrix

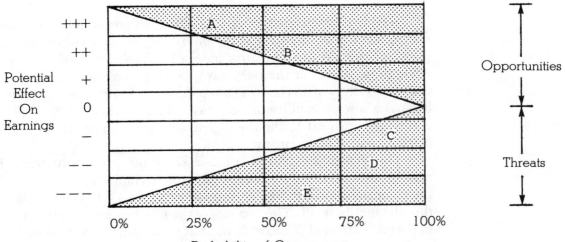

Assessment (Events in shaded areas can have a major impact, while a minor impact is likely to result from events in an unshaded area.)

A. Retail customers like our products, but distribution to this channel is small and unlikely to increase.

B. R&D will continue to generate superior products.

C. Customer tastes may change.

D. Suppliers of raw materials may boost prices faster than inflation.

E. Competition may introduce a new product line.

Having characterized an event as either an opportunity or a threat, management must then assess the probability of its occurrence. Events placed at the left of the matrix have a low probability of occurrence, while those shown at the right have a high probability. Event "A" on the matrix shown in Figure 2–2 represents the strongest opportunity, but has a low probability of occurring. On the other hand, event "E" is the biggest threat facing the organization, and has a greater than 60 percent chance of occurring.

The shaded areas in Figure 2–2 show the prime situations that may be enhanced by an acquisition. For example, in situation "A," the company has found a demand for its products, but penetration in this channel is small. The challenge, then, is to increase market share in the retail channel. This could be done by acquiring a retail distributor, or a company with a sales force well-versed in selling to retailers. In situation "D," the company sees a threat of price increases from its suppliers. The company could buy those same suppliers, or could negotiate long-term contracts with them in an attempt to control price increases.

This example shows why it is important to understand opportunities and threats *before* acquiring. Your acquisition should follow from a careful plan to enhance your company's position or minimize a threat. If you go hunting first, you may seek only those opportunities or threats that rationalize the acquisition.

Another part of forming the corporate profile is assessing your company's strengths and weaknesses to learn whether an acquisition is appropriate.

You should look at strengths and weaknesses not in absolute terms, but in the context of the competition and the marketplace. Compare strengths and weaknesses with those of your competitors. For example, your company may believe its sales force is a strength because sales over the last two years have increased 30 percent. If you later discover that overall industry sales increased by 50 percent over the same time period, your company might have to consider its sales force a weakness instead.

Weigh strengths or weaknesses by the demands of the marketplace. These market needs change over time. Consider changes in the market's needs over time when analyzing your own company or acquisition prospects. There are only limited periods when the needs of a market and the strengths of a firm fit best. Often, this period depends on competitors not entering the same market. For instance, a successful air-freight firm was started by a pilot who routinely shipped drill bit parts from Seattle to Alaska. The pilot decided to use his return flight to bring Alaskan king crabs back to Seattle and to sell them there to restaurants. The demand for fresh crabs proved tremendous. By the time competitors entered the market, the pilot had developed an organization strong enough to approach other, larger markets that the newer, smaller airlines could not serve. The enterprising pilot was able to understand market needs and to see how his strength (unused capacity) could become a success. The key is to understand your firm's strengths and weaknesses *in relationship to the marketplace.*

In searching for acquisition prospects, look for companies that will increase your company's strength in areas that are most important to the marketplace. Top management should participate in the assessment of strengths and weaknesses, although planning can be bottom-up or top-down.

Figure 2–3 shows how to evaluate your firm's strengths and weaknesses. The first column lists certain attributes. In the second column, each of the firm's strengths is ranked compared to the competition. (In this example, the company's products and quality are ranked very strong (5) compared to the competition.) In the third column you should note the importance of each factor in the marketplace. Weigh each factor as some percentage of 1.00. For instance, a factor weighted at 0.25 is considered more important to the marketplace than one weighted at 0.05. These weights may vary from company to company, even from one time to another. In the fourth column, combine the strengths and marketplace factors by multiplying the previous two columns. If all the weighted factors in Figure 2–3 are added (as shown in column 4), we come up with 3.70—which puts this company close to the "strong" category.

The figures in column 4 represent the dynamic relationship of the company's strengths, weighted by the importance of each factor in the marketplace. Once you choose marketplace weights, go to work on the more important factors. For example, Figure 2–3 shows that the two most important factors are: B. Organization and personnel, and E. Marketing and selling capabilities. Both of these factors are rated at 0.25. Understanding this, the company should increase its strengths in these areas.

ASSESSING YOUR ABILITY TO ACQUIRE This is the second part of the corporate profile. Though acquiring another company may seem wise, your company may not be ready to take that step. You must assess this from two viewpoints: financial and managerial. The financial assessment is aimed primarily at finding whether your company is strong enough financially to acquire another firm. The managerial assessment focuses on the ability of your company

Figure 2–3. Evaluation of Strengths and Weaknesses

	Company's Relative Strength	Importance of This Factor in the Marketplace	Overall Assessment
A. Products and product quality	5	0.15	0.75
B. Organization and personnel	4	0.25	1.00
C. Financial capabilities	4	0.10	0.40
D. Operations and physical distribution	5	0.15	0.75
E. Marketing and selling capabilities	2	0.25	0.50
F. Costs and how they are changing with time	4	0.05	0.20
G. Dealers and distribution channels	2	0.05	0.10
Totals:		1.00	3.70

Company's relative strength: 5 = very strong
4 = strong
3 = average
2 = weak
1 = very weak

to successfully absorb another without overdiluting management talent.

In analyses of this sort, it is often beneficial to consider a worst-case scenario based on the following items:

- Drain on capital
- Debt structure
- Loss of board control
- Effect of key managers spending little time on their current activities
- Culture shock for both organizations
- Customer relations

By developing this risk scenario, you can evaluate more objectively the feasibility of the acquisition and identify roadblocks to a successful integration.

The first step in determining your financial ability is to find out how your company intends to pay for the acquisition. Will you use cash, liquidate assets or investments, increase debt, exchange stock, or attempt a ''leveraged buyout'' (using the seller's assets as collateral)? In choosing a form of payment, you can determine how much your company can afford to pay.

Once you select payment alternatives and set a limit on cost, you will be able to determine realistically the size of the acquisition you can make. When you have identified specific candidates for acquisition, you should prepare current and projected *pro forma* financial statements and ratios for the combined entity. The usual period for projection is eighteen months to five years. See Chapter 6 for more information on evaluating candidates in detail.

You must also assess management depth within your own company. One of the biggest threats in any acquisition is dilution of management talent. It is important, before completing any acquisition, to know who will be running the acquired company. Will present management stay? Who will act as liaison between the parent and the new subsidiary? How much time do managers at the parent company have available? If key managers are asked to dedicate half time away from their current activities, would their effectiveness be sharply reduced? Generally, managers who are tackling demanding programs or who are managing distressed departments are not good candidates for taking on the additional responsibility of an acquisition.

This part of the corporate profile is essential to further analysis. If you don't objectively review your ability to manage a potentially risky investment, you may waste time analyzing companies that you cannot acquire, or even worse, acquiring a company that you cannot support properly.

In summary, the corporate profile assesses threats and opportunities and evaluates your company's financial and managerial capability to acquire. With this profile, you can go on to develop the corporate mission.

2.3 DEFINING THE CORPORATE MISSION

Your corporation's mission defines the scope of your acquisition program. It defines the business your company is currently in, sets the tone for the company, and establishes its goals. Your statements of mission should define product areas that you consider primary. The challenge in writing the mission statement lies in defining the character of your company to describe the business accurately while not overly limiting strategic choices.

For example, a large producer of paper towels and tissues defined itself as being in the business of moisture absorption instead of the paper business. By doing so, the company did not limit its horizons to paper products. Company managers realized that their strength was in the technology of designing and distributing moisture-absorption products. With this broader perspective, they could look for companies that dealt with moisture-absorbing materials other than paper.

The corporate mission, especially as it relates to future plans for growth, is an important decision. Therefore, the CEO should have overall responsibility for developing the corporate mission. The CEO may develop the corporate mission with members of the planning department and key executives from areas such as marketing, production, and finance.

2.4 SETTING CORPORATE GOALS AND OBJECTIVES

Corporate goals and objectives set direction; they are statements that fulfill the corporate mission. You should weigh every potential acquisition against these goals. If a candidate is not consistent with your goals, *do not consider it any further.*

Objectives are broad statements; goals are more specific and measurable. Goals refer to specific achievements to be realized within a finite period. For example, an objective (see Figure 2–4) might be to maximize return-on-investment (R.O.I.). A corresponding goal (see Figure 2–5) might be to reach an after-tax R.O.I. of 10 percent within three years.

As shown in Figure 2–5, objectives specify a general direction for the corporation in various areas. It is important to state your own objectives, so that you can compare them with those of candidates and decide whether the objectives are compatible.

Corporate goals, on the other hand, usually are used to set standards for comparing candidates before contacting a target company. For example, corporate goals assist the buyer in screening candidates within an industry. A company whose goal is to expand within its industry and attain an R.O.I. of 10 percent most likely would not be interested in a company with a 5 percent R.O.I. and limited growth prospects. When companies cannot satisfy their goals by finding attractive candidates within the same industry, they may decide to diversify outside their industry.

2.5 DEVELOPING AN INDUSTRY PROFILE

The industry profile begins by identifying sources of information. The better your information, the better your analysis will be. Locate several reliable sources so that you can verify the information. Gather information from within your company, from government sources, and from other public and private sources. Figure 2–6 lists numerous sources. Once you have located sources, you are ready to analyze your own industry. This is like investigating any target industry, though you should presumably be able to analyze your own industry more clearly than other industries.

Your primary objective in analyzing your own industry is to assess its "attractiveness" (versus that of other industries) and to determine your position in the industry. Attractiveness is a relative measure of qualities and trends that mark an industry as worthy of investment.

Figure 2–7 is a checklist for assessing the attractiveness of your own industry and your position within that industry. The checklist is general; you may add or delete items. Four major categories should be consistent between analyses, however. They are:

- Marketing
- Customers
- Competition
- Investment factors

Figure 2–4. Examples of Corporate Objectives*

Financial:
- Survive and avoid bankruptcy
- Become and remain profitable
- Maximize return on investment
- Increase cash flow
- Reduce debt
- Pay dividends
- Increase the dividend payout
- Avoid a takeover

Marketing:
- Increase market share
- Become the market leader
- Achieve an international reputation for service and quality
- Overtake a competitor
- Prevent a potential competitor from becoming significant

Production:
- Improve manufacturing efficiency
- Reduce operating costs
- Improve capacity utilization
- Smooth out production swings
- Maintain full employment

Personnel:
- Increase the percentage of employees who participate in the ownership and profits of the company
- Reduce employee turnover
- Improve the skill level of production workers
- Raise the professionalism of the staff
- Improve morale
- Stabilize relations with unions
- Avoid work stoppages

Social:
- Provide employment for area residents
- Provide goods and services that are useful and not hazardous to the health and welfare of consumers

---

* Adapted from: *Strategic Planning Management*, Thomas H. Naylor, Planning Executives Institute, 1980.

- Minimize conflicts with area residents
- Enhance the corporate image

Political
- Reduce the likelihood of additional government regulations
- Minimize the chances of nationalization of company properties
- Encourage a political climate favorable to business
- Avoid the use of bribes and other illegal means of influencing government actions
- Encourage democratic institutions
- Encourage trade barriers

Figure 2–5. Examples of Corporate Goals*

Financial:
- Achieve a return on sales of 15% by 1987
- Achieve an R.O.I. of 10% by 1986
- Achieve a current ratio of at least 2.0 next year
- Increase earnings per share by at least 25% per year
- Pay a dividend of $1 per share beginning in 1986
- Acquire a particular company in 1987

Marketing:
- Obtain a market share of at least 50% by 1987
- Introduce products into the United Kingdom and Scandinavia by 1986
- Reduce client complaints by 20% in 1986
- Increase total sales volume by 15% next year

Production:
- Reduce excess capacity by 5% next year
- Reduce inventories by 10% in 1987
- Reduce operating costs by 15% by 1986
- Reduce the cost of raw materials by 10% by 1987

Personnel:
- Avoid a strike in 1986
- Eliminate the causes of wildcat strikes
- Reduce employee absenteeism by 5% in 1986
- Reduce employee turnover by 7% by 1987
- Increase the number of professionals with MBA degrees by 15 by 1987

Social:
- Eliminate air and water pollution from a major production facility
- Increase in-house testing of all of the company's products that could potentially be cancer-causing
- Increase the hiring of minorities by at least 10%

Political:
- Voice support for the President's energy program
- Comply with voluntary wage-price guidelines
- Advocate improved strategic planning for all levels of government

---

* Adapted from: *Strategic Planning Management*, Thomas H. Naylor, Planning Executives Institute, 1980.

26

Figure 2–6. Sources of Industry Profile Information

A. Industry Data from Within Your Company:
- Internal market research
- Interviews with salespeople
- Customer correspondence
- Customer complaints

B. Industry Data from the Government:
- Business census data
- Federal publications
- Regulatory agency filings and publications

C. Other Outside Industry Data Sources:
- Existing customers
  - —Interviews with customers
  - —General analysis
- Computerized databases
- Trade associations
- Trade shows
- Trade publications
- Chamber of Commerce
- Outside market-research publications
  - —Industry analysts
  - —Market research organizations
- Telephone book (Yellow Pages)
  - —Firms in your geographic area
- Specialized directories
- Public utilities
- Professional organizations
- Economic-development organizations
- Competitors' literature
  - —Annual reports
  - —Sales brochures
- Suppliers
- Other publications
  - —The *Wall Street Journal*
  - —*Forbes*
  - —*Barrons*
  - —The *Financial Times*
  - —Dun & Bradstreet

- Key Business Ratios
- Robert Morris Associates
- Annual statement studies
  - Ulrich's International Periodicals Directory
  - Predicasts, Inc.
  - F&S Index of Corporations and Industries
  - The *Marketing Information Guide*
  - *Kelley's Manufacturers and Merchants Directory*
  - *Fraser's Canadian Trade Directory*

Figure 2–7. Industry Attractiveness and Business Position Checklist

INDUSTRY ATTRACTIVENESS	BUSINESS POSITION

A. Marketing

_____1. Major market channels in the industry

_____ 1. Market channel currently being serviced by your company

_____2. Size of the whole industry

- In units
- In dollars

_____ 2. Your market share

- In units
- In dollars

_____3. Size of primary market channels

_____3a. Your market share in primary channels

_____3b. Your resource allocation to each primary channel

- Advertising budget
- Number and quality of sales force
- Number of products suited to the channel

_____4. Industry unit growth rate for the last five years

- Total industry
- Primary market segments

_____ 4. Your unit growth rate for the last five years

- Aggregate
- Primary market segments

_____5. Seasonal trends for the industry

_____ 5. Your unit's seasonal trends

_____6. Industry reaction to overall nationwide cycles

_____ 6. Your tendency to lead or lag industry sales trends

_____7. Number of suppliers to the industry

_____ 7. The number of your suppliers

B. Customers (End Users)

_____1. Customers for the products and services of the industry

- Demographics of customer base
  —age distribution
  —income level
  —geographical distribution
  —occupation
  —education level
- Psychographics of customer base
  —price sensitivity
  —buyer behavior (usage rate, loyalty benefits sought, etc.)
  —attitudes on product quality

_____ 1. Your influence over your customers

29

_____2. Size of the customer base

_____3. Growth trend of the customer base

C. Competition

_____1. Competitors in the industry

_____2. Characteristics of the competition

_____ 2. The characteristics of your organization compared to all competitors

- Current market share and changes over the last three years
- Quality of products and services
- Earnings and sales trends
- Profits
- Geographic segmentation
- Marketing capability
- Production strength
- Financial capability
- Consumer acceptance
- Management

_____3. Degree of horizontal, forward, and backward integration used by each competitor

_____ 3. Your degree of integration

_____4. Number of new competitors over the last five years

_____5. Number of competitors who have left the industry over the last five years

_____6. Market strategies of the leading competitors

_____ 6. Your market strategies

_____7. Nature of competition within the industry

- Service
- Price
- Quality
- Advertising
- Other

_____8. Marketing approach of major competitors

- Consumer marketing programs
- Distribution methods
- Field sales approach
- Product mix

_____ 8. Your marketing approach

_____9. Barriers to competitive entry in the industry
- Patents held
- Large capital investment required
- Economies of scale
- Technical expertise
- Brand name loyalty
- Product differentiation
- Complexity
- Other

_____ 9. Your competitive advantages

D. Investment Factors

_____1. Industry performance over the last five years

- Stock prices
- P/E ratios
- Industry profit margins
- Investment efficiency
  —return on total assets
  —return on equity capital
  —stock price as a percent of book value

_____ 1. Your company's performance over the last five years

_____2. Major developments likely to affect the industry

- Regulatory
- Economic
- Social
- Technological

_____ 2. Your company's ability to cope with change

31

The marketing analysis consists of detailing key statistics and trends for the industry and your position within industry norms. It includes quantifying the size and growth of the market and defining major channels of the industry.

The purpose of the customer analysis is to understand who are the customers. How many customers are there? What are their attitudes? What is the growth trend? This analysis sometimes is important in locating candidates for acquisition who are serving the same kinds of customers in different geographic locations. Understand your own customers first.

Next, analyze your competition. Understanding your competition can help you decide whether you should expand in your own industry or explore other opportunities.

The final category consists of investment performance factors commonly used by investors to evaluate an industry or a company. This analysis gives you an objective picture of your industry and its prospects. An objective review allows all potential buyers to see how others view them, particularly prospective sellers.

2.6 SELECTING A GROWTH STRATEGY

Developing the corporate growth strategy naturally follows the steps developed in this chapter. In the process of developing a corporate profile, defining your mission, setting goals and objectives, and developing an industry profile, you will uncover sources for growth strategies. You should note these ideas. The fifth step is to select a growth strategy. Remember that growth strategy need not focus solely on acquisition. Consider acquisition one of many choices in your company's growth plan.

SOURCES OF ACQUISITION STRATEGIES Your most important source of growth strategies is your analysis of where your company is, where you want it to go, and its growth prospects. An obvious source for an acquisition strategy is your review of the company's strengths and weaknesses. You may choose to acquire another firm to make up for a weakness within your own company or to gain a particular strength from another firm. For example, one company found that its distribution network was inadequate to meet sales targets in its fast-growing industry. To overcome this weakness, it acquired another company in the industry which it judged to have the best dealer relationships in the industry.

Reviewing opportunities and threats is another source of ideas on growth strategies. By being aware of opportunities, many corporations have been able to grow by acquiring companies that fit their long-term needs. Meeting long-term needs is the important ingredient in this strategy. Many firms acquire because they feel the low price of a candidate represents an opportunity. The price of the candidate should never be the overriding rationale for acquisition. Although price is important, consider the strategic "fit" your first priority. You can properly assess the strategic fit only when you understand your company's mission, objectives, and goals.

It is equally important to understand threats to your company. In this strategy, your company may acquire another to lessen some existing or potential threat. There is an interesting example in the communications industry. A large communications firm threatened an unfriendly takeover of a small electronics company. To defend itself from the unwanted tender offer, the smaller company acquired a local radio station. The large communications company then was accused of restraint-of-trade because it sought to buy a firm that had holdings in the same industry.

The industry profile also yields valuable insights on possible acquisition strategies. Knowing your industry has a direct bearing on your company's strategy for acquisitions. If the analysis shows that your industry promises strong future growth, you may consider acquiring firms in your own industry. You could do this by any of the following means:

- Acquiring a firm that supplies you (*backward integration*).
- Acquiring a firm that distributes your products (*forward integration*).
- Acquiring a firm that competes in the same marketplace (*horizontal integration*). Antitrust problems have to be taken into account here.

If your industry does not show a strong potential for growth, or if other industries appear to have better potential, you may prefer to acquire outside your industry. There are two types of diversification: horizontal and conglomerate diversification. *Horizontal diversification* means acquiring a firm to form synergistic benefits by matching your strengths to another firm's weaknesses (or vice versa). *Conglomerate or portfolio diversification* is acquiring another firm that is not related to your central business, but which represents an opportunity or promises to offset some deficiency. For example, a company that produces equipment for buildings, and wishes to offset cyclical swings, might be interested in acquiring an electronics company that does defense

Figure 2–8. Acquisition Strategies Resulting from the Industry Analysis

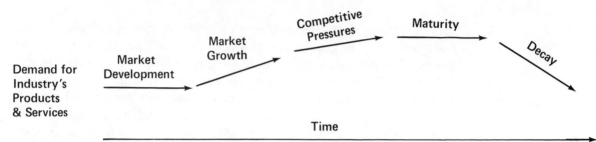

Industry Outlook	Uncertain	Excellent	Good	OK	Poor
Generalized M&A Growth Strategies	Stay at Home	Integrative Growth • Backward • Forward • Horizontal		Diversified Growth • Horizontal	Conglomerate Growth and/or Divestiture
Marketing Objectives	Develop Awareness for Product & Services	Establish Strong Market Position	Establish Competitive Advantages	Increase/Defend Present Market Position	Look to New Industries & Consolidate Services

work for the government. In this way, the company is less likely to be hurt if the construction industry becomes depressed. Figure 2–8 shows a generalized acquisition strategy over the cycle of demand for a company's products.

Other ideas may come from your review of competition in your industry. Counteracting your competition's moves by acquiring can promote long-term growth. Recent examples of this can be found in the financial industry, where firms are matching one another in forming multiservice organizations through acquisition.

ALTERNATIVES TO ACQUISITION

Because of the inherent risk, cost, and time commitment involved, you should consider acquisition only one of the choices available to you in planning growth. Other alternatives include: internal growth, joint ventures, licensing agreements, supplier agreements, trademark agreements, and simply doing nothing.

- **Internal Growth:** The company grows by allocating its resources to high-growth areas within the firm. The key factors here are timing and cost. Internal growth is usually slower than growth through acquisition. How attractive is the new venture? Is there time to build from within, or are competitors planning to move into this business in the near future? Might the cost of plant, equipment, and product development be cheaper than an acquisition?

- **Joint Ventures:** Two firms may go into business together. Joint ventures usually are temporary agreements, although some have lasted more than fifty years. The distinguishing feature of a joint venture is shared management. Managers from both partners oversee the new venture. While many joint ventures are successful, conflict may arise between the partners. The primary rationale for most joint ventures is new markets for mature products or access to raw materials. The two firms do not necessarily have to have equal ownership in the venture. One party could reduce its investment by having a minority interest.

- **Licensing Agreements:** Licensing new ideas from other companies, independent inventors, or the government is a common growth strategy. Inventors or companies are typically willing to sell their rights to a product, idea, or process when they consider the market too small to develop, when they want to concentrate their resources in another area, or when they lack the capital to develop the market.

- **Supplier Agreements:** If you are considering acquiring one of your suppliers to control your supply sources, you also should consider negotiating a long-term sole-source agreement. This agreement could help stabilize prices and may even lower them, and it is far less risky than acquisition.
- **Trademark Agreements:** Buying the rights to another company's trademark is a way to gain instant credibility in a market familiar with that trademark. The risks in these agreements usually lie in control over the product and the fees.
- **Doing Nothing:** As we said, acquisition is a risky way to grow. You should weigh the risk of doing nothing against the risk of an acquisition.

COMMON REASONS FOR CHOOSING ACQUISITION

Since there are many alternatives among which to choose, make certain acquisition is best for your situation. Justify any acquisition with a valid business reason. Atlhough acquiring may satisfy a short-term need, the ultimate purpose should be to promote long-term growth and profitability.

Express reasons for an acquisition in strategic or operational terms such as:

1. Gain better distribution
2. Offset product obsolescence
3. Get better access to raw materials suppliers and restrain price increases
4. Improve cyclical and seasonal stability
5. Develop economies of scale
6. Improve the effectiveness of the marketing effort
7. Get advanced technology
8. Acquire managerial talent
9. Improve credit position
10. Acquire additional products that complement existing products
11. Obtain needed plant and equipment
12. Use slack capacity

There is no one way to choose "the right strategy." Your selection should be based on insight and research.

SELECTING THE APPROPRIATE GROWTH STRATEGY

In selecting a growth strategy, measure all choices against some criteria to help develop management consensus on which direction to take. Here are some common criteria:

- Is the acquisition strategy consistent with the way in which the company has operated in the past years?
- Does the strategy respond to expected changes in the industry?
- Is the strategy practical?
    —What is the level of risk?
    —Do you have the resources you need to acquire (capital, management)?
    —Does the strategy conform with your company's standards?
    —What return on investment is required?

Figure 2–8 is a useful checklist summarizing the acquisition strategy, its goals, and criteria for its selection.

Once you have selected an acquisition strategy and management clearly understands its direction, you are ready to look for candidates. Chapter 3 discusses more specifically how to find and screen potential candidates.

Figure 2–9. Acquisition Strategy Checklist

1. Describe the acquisition strategy:

   _____

   _____

2. What is the objective of this strategy?

   _____

   _____

3. What are the goals for this strategy?
   (Quantify expected results and set deadlines)

   _____

   _____

4. Describe the criteria for choosing this acquisition strategy:

   • To capitalize on strengths (describe them)

   _____

   • To overcome weaknesses (describe them)

   _____

   • To exploit opportunities (describe them)

   _____

   • To lessen threats (describe them)

   _____

   • To counter competition (describe circumstances)

   _____

Finding and
Screening
Candidates

3

3.1 INTRODUCTION

You are in charge of a merger and acquisition program. You have taken the first step—developing a profile of your own company. You know your own strengths and weaknesses, and you've assessed available resources, both human and financial.

With that profile in hand, you're ready to find and make a first-cut evaluation of candidates for an acquisition or merger. That field of candidates, just as would a field of political candidates, must be narrowed. This chapter covers both steps in more detail.

3.2 FINDING CANDIDATES

In a recent survey of corporate directors by Touche Ross & Co., the difficulty of finding good candidates was mentioned twice as often as any other deterrent to merger. Why are good candidates so hard to find? Certainly companies everywhere are for sale. But many of these companies are failing or clearly headed for failure. In its initial stages, the search calls for keen judgment. This means identifying and prioritizing areas to review. Not all areas should be viewed equally.

The essence of finding candidates is to look carefully, yet not too carefully. Begin screening only after you have compiled a list of candidates. But don't waste time by making that list indiscriminately. Inevitably, finding candidates involves at least a cursory screening.

Many of the luckiest acquisitions result from informal contacts and casual tips. But it pays to do your own sleuthing as well. The following is a list of sources you can use to find candidates:

1. Contact through other business activity
2. Walk in and introduce yourself
3. Chamber of Commerce directories
4. Trade associations
5. Placing and/or reading advertisements
6. Reading business news
7. Business brokers
8. Using computerized financial information databases
9. Commercial real estate brokers
10. Consultants
11. Bank trust officers
12. Commercial loan officers
13. Securities firms
14. Public accounting firms
15. Law firms
16. Small Business Administration
17. Factoring companies
18. Venture capitalists
19. Personal acquaintances
20. Insurance brokers and agents

Here are some of the things you should look for as you scan those sources:

- A corporation whose largest shareholders are near retirement may be a likely candidate.
- A corporation advertising for a new chief executive officer.
- Any public announcements from corporations on new strategic directions for the company.

- A public company with an important position in a growing industry segment.

- A closely held corporation whose largest shareholder wishes to sell to make his or her estate more easily divisible.

- A company started one to three years ago may be running low on enthusiasm and capital. The owner may offer to stay on as manager, giving you the company and an experienced person to run it.

- Partners who vary too greatly in age or disposition may wish to sell to avoid disruptions.

- Companies that generate a lot of cash may cause tax disadvantages.

These are but a few of the situations that can make owners receptive to an offer to acquire. Your best bet is homework: the more avenues you pursue (at this early step), however improbable, the better your chances of discovering good but inconspicuous candidates, of unearthing candidates worthy of further scrutiny.

3.3 SETTING CRITERIA

Now you must use the information you have gathered to establish criteria against which to measure acquisition candidates. Using your own company's criteria to assess other companies is a key factor in determining the potential for synergistic benefits to be derived from the merger. How you set criteria is important in another way: make criteria too broad, and you will wind up with too many candidates; make them too stringent, and few companies will meet them.

Keep in mind the fact that a merger and acquisition program is not a short-term growth strategy. The objective of the screening process described in this chapter and the next is to identify candidates with qualities that are most likely to benefit your company. It could be a mistake to acquire a company just to gain market clout or to control resources. You must consider your own firm's long-term strategy.

This chapter introduces the first two steps in the three-level approach shown in Figure 3–1. Chapter 4 will discuss Level III screening.

Using this approach saves both time and resources as it helps to uncover suitable candidates.

Level I screening is an initial "go/no-go" analysis performed on all candidates. This step ultimately eliminates 80 percent of the original group, which might have included an entire industry segment (databases available today may be used to easily identify such groups).

Level II screening ranks companies according to how well they meet your company's selection criteria. This process eliminates approximately three fourths of the remaining candidates.

Level III screening, which is detailed in Chapter 4, is an in-depth quantitative and qualitative analysis used to make your final selection.

Although criteria must be identified and used throughout the screening process, you should be willing to relax them on occasion if an unusual opportunity comes along. You may also have to find a way to fit the cost of a deal within the established criteria. For instance, if you lack the resources needed to see a merger through, you may be able to find a partner to help you finance the deal.

The screening process described in this chapter formalizes the selection of suitable candidates for merger and acquisition. It does so by first drawing up a candidate profile that details desirable criteria—type of business, type of products, size, location, and so forth. As previously stated, the scope of these criteria determines the size of the universe from which you will ultimately make your choice. If criteria are too specific, your universe will be small. Make criteria too general and there will be many prospects, thus making subsequent screening both lengthy and expensive.

Some factors used to construct a candidate profile may appear to be in conflict and will require you to make compromises. As problems are resolved, a realistic image emerges. Once identified, criteria can serve the following purposes:

- Consolidate agreement within your own organization
- Reaffirm your own corporate goals and strategies
- Form the core of the "want ad" package you will be distributing as you initiate the search
- Help focus your search on valid candidates

The next section looks more closely at Level I activities, the first step in the screening process.

Figure 3–1. The Screening Process

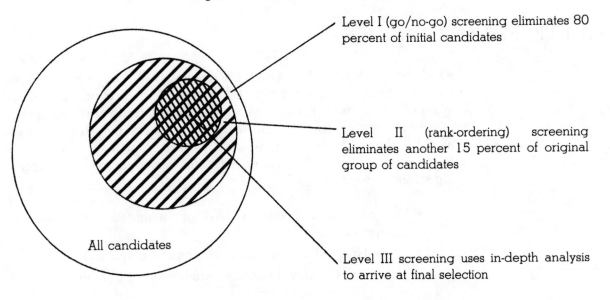

Level I (go/no-go) screening eliminates 80 percent of initial candidates

Level II (rank-ordering) screening eliminates another 15 percent of original group of candidates

Level III screening uses in-depth analysis to arrive at final selection

All candidates

3.4 LEVEL I SCREENING

As shown in Figure 3–1, Level I screening is a "go/no-go" analysis used to eliminate approximately 80 percent of the original candidates. Ways of automating this process are described later in this chapter.

In the initial stages of your search, you must establish the bounds of the universe from which suitable candidates will be selected. As expected, these are fairly broad criteria. Some examples of actual screening statements follow:

- The search should concentrate on opportunities in the following businesses:
  —Hospital and scientific equipment manufacturers
  —High-volume household products (not durables) of metal, plastic, wood, or glass
  —Leisure products
- The search should consider investment opportunities ranging up to a total of $40 million.

Once you have developed your own company's profile, you have in fact created the benchmarks or criteria against which to compare candidates for acquisition. You want to single out companies with qualities that can help you and that are in concert with your company's long-term strategy. Here are some common screening criteria:

- Sales and earnings growth equal to or greater than your own company's (to improve your company's growth)
- The size of the market you are targeting (and its direction)
- A need to access established distribution channels

One common pitfall is the tendency to spend too much time on individual candidates in the early stages of the search. At this point, you must focus on fundamental issues and quickly weed out obvious losers.

A checklist similar to that shown in Figure 3–2 can help speed the process. You may weigh certain factors, so that even one or two check marks on the minus side will suffice to eliminate a candidate.

Every search must be individualized. A minor requirement in one search may become critical in another. For instance, geographic location may not be crucial in a highly decentralized organization. But if synergy

Figure 3–2. Sample Level I Checklist

Candidate: _____   RATING CHECKLIST

_____

Owner: _____   Product(s): _____

_____   Approx. Value: $ _____

	poor			good	
	−2	−1	0	+1	+2
• Willingness to sell				X	
• Desirability of product line					X
• Customer profile				X	
• Market potential					X
• Suitability of location		X			
• Condition of plant and equipment		X			
• Assessment of competition				X	
• Assessment of growth potential					X
• Assessment of personnel picture				X	
• Assessment of financial history					
• Assessment of management					
• Profitability					

depends on shared functions and common distribution channels, a plant's location could prove to be very significant.

Another key aspect of eliminating losers is the ability to spot traps and pitfalls. Some operations simply cannot be turned around. As a general policy, except for very few circumstances, stay away from a company that has consistently lost money—no matter how attractive its price tag.

You obviously should examine whatever financial records may be available. But there are less tangible, yet equally important factors. For example, a company's success may depend on its owner's know-how and connections. Without that individual the business could be severely impacted.

Another area to explore is the owner's motive for making a deal. Although there are lots of "respectable" reasons for wanting to sell a business (retirement, illness, and so forth), you will find the seller less likely to mention others. These may include such things as new zoning laws or government regulations that are going to cut into profits, the loss of key employees, obsolete technology or equipment, pending law-suits, disappearing markets or sources of raw materials, and literally dozens of other scenarios that could turn a bargain into a nightmare. Look for early hints of trouble and move quickly to eliminate doubtful prospects. Level II screening will check out every candidate in greater detail.

Level I screening must be a routine, mechanical process. You may be checking an entire industry segment, and you simply don't have time to do more than compare a candidate against your initial criteria. If you wish to speed the process, you can include more specific require-ments, such as a candidate's minimum return on invested capital, mini-mum potential growth, or minimum overall size. Section 3.6 shows how Level 1 screening can be automated.

No matter how broad or specific your criteria, you must remain true to the fundamental reasons for seeking the merger or acquisition in the first place. The candidate profile you create must help you achieve your overall goal—to penetrate new markets, to diversify, to grow, or whatever.

Specific pricing issues require a great deal of time and effort and are dealt with in detail at the Level III stage covered in Chapter 4. The following, however, are some financial issues to be considered now:

- What is the company worth? (What are its assets worth, com-pared to its purchase price?) Is the price fair? Is the owner willing to negotiate?

- How much capital must your company invest in the deal? (What return are you looking for in this investment?)

To more clearly show typical evaluation criteria, here is a list taken from a major food manufacturer's initial list:

1. **Preferred area of diversification.** A winemaking enterprise with its own vineyards. The company should have established brands and must do its own blending.
2. **Size of investment.** Approximately 150,000 cases per year (360,000 U.S. gallons), with a sales turnover in the $4–$6 million range.
3. **Product line.** Wines may be red or white, provided they are better quality products (intended to retail at approximately $10 per bottle). If lower-priced wines are included, white wines should predominate.
4. **Preferred location.** California.
5. **Trading ratios.**
   - A stable record that shows net profit after tax in the 20–25 percent range
   - A record of turnover growth in the 10–15 percent range
   - A 35–40 percent ratio of working capital to assets
   - A long-term debt-to-equity ratio in the 25–30 percent range
6. **Terms of acquisition.** A $15–$20 million cash acquisition only (no stock to be offered). Partial acquisition (of 51 percent or more) may be arranged, with agreement to purchase the rest within a specified time period.

The screening profile should serve as a selling tool as well as a blueprint for your search. Here is an example consisting of a goal and a list of attributes designed to sell the parent company to prospective sellers.

OBJECTIVE To select companies, including divisions and/or product lines, in the garden supply and related fields that, if acquired, will provide mutual long-term benefits both to the acquired company and corporation.
Our company offers several benefits to a potential acquisition:

- A proven, successful track record
- A marketable stock listed on the New York Stock Exchange

- A management with in-depth knowledge of the garden supply business
- A strong financial position and the ability to attract both debt and equity capital to ensure financing for growth

As you can see, setting objectives down on paper can serve several purposes. At this point in your search, you have taken an industry segment and compared each company in that segment to the candidate profile established earlier. Using a *quick,* go/no-go approach, you should be able to come up with a list of prospects approximately one fifth the size of your original list.

Now proceed to the next step, Level II screening, in which you will eliminate approximately three fourths of the remaining candidates.

3.5 LEVEL II SCREENING

You are about to narrow the field of potential candidates down to a final few. The ultimate selection is quite detailed and will be discussed in the next chapter. This section describes the process used to develop a composite evaluation by weighting the remaining candidates against common selection criteria. Figure 3–3 illustrates typical Level II screening criteria. You will require different criteria for every search.

In many respects, this step resembles Level I screening. It's just that now you can go a bit further in quantifying the degree to which a candidate matches your expectations. Level II screening uses your intuitive judgment about the value of criteria that you have identified. It breaks down your best guess and attaches a value to how each candidate measures up to those criteria. It forces you to get down to specifics, but it does so without taking up a lot of your valuable time.

The basic objective of Level II screening is simple—to refine the list of potential candidates by weighing the criteria and applying those weighted criteria against companies that made it through your first screen. But at this point you still can't afford to spend a great deal of time looking at individual candidates. That must wait until Level III screening.

3.6 AUTOMATED SCREENING

Screening has been made a great deal simpler thanks to the availablity of databases that allow you to look at thousands of companies in a

Figure 3–3. Level II Screening Process*

Screening Criteria	Weight of Criteria	Company A		Company B		Company C		Company D	
		CS	W	CS	W	CS	W	CS	W
5-year annual compound rate of growth:									
Sales (greater than 15%)	3	1	3	1	3	1	3		
Earnings (greater than 15%)	3	2	6	−1	−3	1	3	(etc.)	
Position in industry (shows leadership)	2	2	4	0	0	1	2		
Size of potential market (greater than $100 million)	2	1	2	1	2	2	4		
Marketing channels to supermarkets and drug stores	1	0	0	1	1	1	1		
Strong research capability	1	2	2	1	1	1	1		
.	.	.	.	.	.	.	.		
.	.	.	.	.	.	.	.		
.	.	.	.	.	.	.	.		
(etc.)									

Company Criteria Status (CS):

  2 Exceeds criteria or possesses a very desirable trait
  1 Meets screening criteria
  0 No advantage or detriment shown in this area
−1 Does not meet screening criteria
−2 This trait is detrimental to our company

* Note that criteria have been weighted equally among candidates. In addition, each candidate's status (listed in column CS) is then multiplied by the weight of the criteria to give its weighted total (listed in column W).

matter of minutes. One of the better known listings covers nearly 150,000 companies.

These databases may be searched (for a fee, of course) through the services of several financial service corporations. Many professional merger and acquisition consultants also have their own proprietary data bases. Touche Ross, for example, has an automated data base with over 500 expressed sellers and buyers. They are particularly useful to generate the initial universe of all companies from which you will eventually select your candidates. By requesting a list of all companies with a specific Standard Industrial Classification (SIC) code, you can narrow your search to a specific industry segment.

Databases can also help you perform Level I screening tasks. They allow you to impose various combinations of constraints as you generate successive subsets of your original list. Available databases typically include the following information:

- Company name and address
- NYSE/ASE/OTC ticker symbol (unless company is privately owned)
- SIC Code
- Number of employees
- Annual sales volume
- Net income
- Market value
- P/E ratio
- Earnings history

Starting with an entire industry group (using primary or secondary SIC), you can narrow the field by imposing whatever financial and geographic constraints you wish to include. For example, the following questions may be answered:

- What are all the companies in my area with sales of $3 million or more?
- Which of these companies have market-to-book ratios that are less than 1?
- Which of these companies have a return on equity greater than 12 percent?
- Which of these companies show an earnings-per-share growth of 5 percent or more over the past five years?

Subsets may be generated separately or successively. As files are created and transferred to your terminal, you may weigh criteria and do preliminary Level II screening on some companies. But private companies do not have to report detailed financial information. As a result, database coverage for such companies is only suitable for Level I screening.

In summary, databases allow you to do in-depth financial analyses of a great many companies (particularly public corporations) in a very short time.

Detailed Analysis
and Evaluation

4

4.1 INTRODUCTION

By this stage of the merger process, you will have developed a realistic profile of your own company. Knowing what to look for, you established criteria and cut the list of candidates down to five percent or so of its original size. The remaining candidates appear to share qualities most likely to assist your company in achieving its long-range objectives.

This chapter describes what I call Level III screening, which is an in-depth analysis that will lead to a final selection. Level III screening enables you to make the final decision on a candidate.

There is no way to be absolutely sure that a company does not have hidden flaws. Level I and II screening will reveal most obvious problems. But you must perform Level III screening to discover the things that *might* go wrong: overstated inventories, obsolete plant, or impending shortages, for example. Also, you'll want to look for opportunities: an unexplored market, perhaps a sleeper. It's important to look both ways.

As we noted in Chapter 1, most business mergers result in failure. No study can guarantee that this will not happen to you. But against such odds, you'll want to know a lot about your candidates before making a serious commitment.

Each candidate must be vigorously scouted. What's management like? How does the company stand in its own industry? How do the figures look? Are the employees stable and productive? How are the company's relations with labor, customers, and suppliers?

This kind of scouting should not be asked of people responsible for acquiring and planning. You can't very well be suitor and critic at once. Your own corporate development people may feel pressured to push any candidate through just to show they've done something. You'll need an objective group whose incentives are not based on the outcome of the evaluation.

The more time you have to evaluate the candidates, the more you can avoid surprises. But there's a trade-off. You may have to move quickly—to win the seller's confidence, to stay ahead of competing buyers, to arrange financing. Use your best judgment to decide when you've studied in enough depth. Remember that there are some things you can't review. Some details and subtleties will emerge only later. Your task, basically, is to separate large and chronic problems from small and acute ones.

Much of this chapter will describe specific risks and opportunities you should look for. But first, two strategies are introduced for your review. One is the acquisition audit—a selective audit performed to check the reliability of the seller's financial status and records. The second, a business review, is a comprehensive study of the company's four most important resources: finance, products, marketing, and people.

An acquisition audit helps you to convince yourself that your estimates of the target's finances are reliable. If the company's records are not certified, your risk increases. You may want to employ a CPA firm to do an acquisition audit. For this special-purpose audit, the accountant will not test all accounts and will not offer a certified opinion, but will instead save time and money by testing only key accounts.

But note, even a review of certified financial statements may not yield enough information to investigate a candidate properly. When looking at the financials, keep in mind:

1. Assets generally are reported at cost, understating their value in times of inflation.

2. Intangible assets (such as patents and contracts) and certain liabilities (such as leases, contracts, and legal claims) may not show up on the balance sheet.

3. Elective inventory methods may make it difficult to compare the target company's reported assets and operating results with those of your company or others in the industry.

You must remember that a certified audit and—to a lesser extent—an acquisition audit, though valuable in confirming accounts, is not intended to be a broad-based examination of all the company's business affairs. The business review helps uncover these matters. The purpose of the business review is to identify corporate issues that would be of concern to a potential buyer or seller, over and above testing the accuracy of certain financial statement accounts.

The business review will give you a detailed understanding of the operational and financial traits of your candidates. By studying each company's history, products, operations, competition, properties, personnel, and finances, you may uncover features as well as faults. Expertise in analyzing a business combination from the viewpoint of taxation, operations, accounting, auditing, and SEC matters is needed in a thorough business review.

Your review may be impeded by the following:

1. The seller naturally will hesitate to risk the discretion of employees, suppliers, customers, and brokers. The strict secrecy required by the seller may hold you up.

2. If you're courting a competitor, the seller may refuse to disclose proprietary information.

3. Under hostile circumstances (such as Mesa Petroleum's 1984 attempt to acquire Gulf Oil), you will probably get no cooperation from the target, and you may have to rely on public information alone (SEC filings, annual reports, newspapers, and the like).

You may be able to reduce or overcome these problems by signing nondisclosure or conditional-purchase agreements.

4.2 ASSESSING RISK IN THE ACQUISITION

Risk is inherent in any acquisition. It can never be eliminated, no matter how intensely candidates are reviewed. In fact, if you study too long, you may overemphasize a candidate's faults or fall into inaction. The more time you spend on closing the deal, the more likely the parties will get cold feet and walk away from the transaction. However, thoroughness is critical. You can be too thorough, but history suggests you're more likely not to be careful enough.

You must balance your downside risks against the potential for profit; a high potential candidate may justify high risk. Recall the purposes for acquisition we described in Chapter 2—capitalizing on your strengths or reducing your weaknesses. Looking at a candidate in the context of your own company, you may see the chance for synergy. For example, if your company's market is seasonal, you may benefit both companies by acquiring one whose season is countercyclical to yours. To take advantage of a marketing opportunity, your strong production capability might be enhanced by combining with a company that is strong in marketing. If a small market share restrains the growth of your company and that of a competitor, you might both benefit from a merger. So you see, it is not enough to look at a candidate on its own merits. You must estimate what problems and benefits would accrue from the candidate's fit to your own company.

Earnings are affected by controllable factors (such as management actions) and by uncontrollable factors (such as the weather). The more uncontrollable factors a company faces, the greater the risk that earnings will fluctuate or decline.

Risks arise in a company's operations and are affected by the climate in which it operates (political, economic, social, and environmental).

Risks in operations seem endless, but we'll cite some examples. Dependence on key employees, unreliable suppliers, and weak supporting industries may make a company vulnerable.

There are many risks, external to the company, that should be examined. Political risks arise daily. Currencies fluctuate, wars begin and end, legislators have their whims, and so on. You should calculate how much of the candidate's earnings depend on government action—defense contracts, foreign policy, diplomatic incidents, and so forth. For example, American oil companies' earnings obviously are tied to political events in the volatile Middle East. (To compensate for this risk, some companies have diversified into other lines of business or other geographical areas.)

Market risks may arise from a prior legal problem (Ford's Pinto and Firestone's defective tire), political opinions (defense contractors during the Vietnam war), or a poor financial history (the WPPSS default).

Environmental risks are greatest with certain agricultural, manufacturing, and tourism industries. Poor weather can disrupt the sales of everything from summer tours to convertibles. Storms and earthquakes may cause severe losses. Your only protection is to gauge the risks of such events in the area in which your candidate operates and plan to carry adequate insurance.

The risks of eventual bankruptcy should always be assessed. A powerful tool used by Touche Ross & Co. to investigate targets in this regard is called the Touche Ross Early Warning System. This monitoring mechanism is designed to identify in its incipient stages the possibility of failure in a company. The Early Warning System combines organizational, mathematical, financial, statistical, and operations-review techniques in a comprehensive analysis of corporate problems. The results are then processed by computer, measured against the results of other companies, and the probability of future financial difficulties is estimated.

To help you assess risks, the next section of this chapter is devoted to four main areas in which you should evaluate candidates: finance, operations, marketing, and management and personnel. The section ends with a checklist used to make sure you've covered everything.

4.3 FINANCIAL ASSESSMENT

During Level I and II screening, you gathered financial data on candidates. Though data was relatively shallow and the evaluation cursory, it helped you eliminate obvious problems. Now, in Level III screening, you're going to go back over that data and gather new information. You'll be gauging the reliability of reported revenues and expenses, and you'll be looking behind the numbers to see what they mean in everyday terms. Finally, you will calculate ratios to spot imbalances and infer some of management's strategies. It is important to remember that financial statements from company to company are frequently not comparable. Risks can be lessened if you are analyzing statements that have received a favorable opinion from a certified public accounting firm.

INCOME STATEMENT ANALYSIS Candidates who pass Level I and II screening appear to have attractive income statements. Revenues should look strong and expenses should be under control. But the numbers tell only a part of the company's financial health.

To begin, what is the quality of the earnings?

Briefly, you will study the accounting policies and controls of the target company. Conservative and objective accounting practices generally lend greater credibility to its income statement. When the income statement seems to be based on poor records, you must compensate for this to arrive at a reliable picture of the company's situation.

Different accounting policies can produce different earnings results. You can guard against this by comparing the company's income statement and accounting practices with those of other companies in its industry, and by hunting for signs of inconsistent figures. Once found, such figures should be adjusted to comparable practice.

Changes in accounting practices can produce different earnings. For example, if a company changes its inventory valuation policy from LIFO to FIFO, the result would be to boost earnings. Earnings would also decrease if the company moved from a straight line to an accelerated method of depreciation. The analyst should closely examine the timing of costs and revenues.

There are several other ways a company might attempt to manage earnings and construct favorable earnings history. When studying the target company you should check for arbitrary changes in actuarial assumptions in a pension plan that might enhance earnings. The earnings history can be affected by warranty costs that have been deferred or poorly estimated. Over- and underaccrued costs, an acute write-off or "financial bath," and a highly variable relationship between sales and net income are other conditions that should be thoroughly studied.

When you spot artificially inflated or depressed figures, you should correct them, by estimating more accurate figures yourself, and adjust the income statement accordingly. Only then will the statement be more reliable for your purposes.

For example, suppose you note that a candidate has set aside $8 million to cover warranty costs. Your analysis indicates that $6 million would be more reasonable—perhaps the candidate wants an accounting cushion. You should adjust earnings upward by $2 million. Conversely, if the candidate shows a provision for expense of $10 million that you believe should be $16 million, you should adjust the stated income before tax downward by $6 million.

Figure 4–1 is a list of factors that decrease the quality of the candidate's earnings. Study the candidate's income statement for signs of problems such as those described in Figure 4–1. If you find any, estimate their effect on revenues and expenses and correct the net income figure accordingly.

Beyond the numbers in the income statement, however, you must look at the forces and events behind them. Specifically, you'll develop an industry profile for the candidate just as you did for your own company in Chapter 2. (You may wish to review Chapter 2 for a more detailed discussion of the industry profile.) Pay particular attention to sales and to cost of sales.

SALES Define the market segment of the candidate's products or services. How large is this segment? Is it growing or shrinking? Who are the candidate's major competitors? What are their strengths and weaknesses? How is

Figure 4–1. Factors Harmful to Earnings

- Unstable income statement elements not explained by normal business fluctuations

- Earnings determined using liberal accounting methods, resulting in an overstatement of net income. Such an overstatement may also result in the overstatement of projections of future earnings

- Net income based on ultraconservative accounting policies (since the resulting net income is misleading as a basis for predicting future earnings)

- Unreliable and inaccurate accounting estimates

- Earnings smoothed or managed artificially (such as shifting of expenses among reporting periods)

- Deferral of costs without future economic benefit

- Premature or belated revenue recognition

- Underaccrual or overaccrual of expenses

- Unjustified cutback in discretionary costs

the industry affected by external factors—the overall economy, government policy and negotiations, and regional economic dislocations? Each of these segments should be investigated in depth.

Who are the candidate's largest customers? Has there been any significant shift in their respective percentages of company sales within the last five years? Most important, are there signs of impending changes that will affect the customer base?

Perhaps the most critical area is the sales forecast. What is the system for collecting data? Who provides the input? How reliable has it been in the past? How healthy is the candidate's sales backlog? What assumptions about the future behavior of the national economy underlie the sales forecast? Are these assumptions reasonable? If sales appear to be cyclical, step back and look at the sales history again. Are there incurable flaws, such as obsolete products, a declining marketplace, increasing competition, or shrinking margins? Remember that sales forecasts may be overly optimistic.

Your industry profile should begin with the candidate itself (unless, of course, the merger or acquisition would take place under hostile circumstances). Consult key managers. Then gather background material, such as reports from trade associations, banks, and stock brokers. Finally, there is no substitute for talking directly to suppliers, customers, competitors, bankers, and anyone else who knows the industry and is willing to cooperate. Figure 2–6 lists sources of information.

While you're at it, look for opportunities to make the candidate's sales function more efficient. For instance, would the function benefit if you did any of the following:

1. More closely link sales strategy with profitability considerations
2. Improve distribution methods
3. Accelerate order filling and billing
4. Create incentives (interest charges and discounts) for prompt payment

COST OF SALES   The cost of sales is generally divided into three major components: materials, direct labor, and overhead. In each area, study the current situation and look for opportunities for improvements.

Who are the major suppliers? Are there any special contacts, relationships, or agreements that would or would not transfer to you, the buyer? How healthy is the competition in the supplier's industry? What is the cost and availability of labor (skilled and/or unskilled) in the local marketplace? Is labor organized, and if so, does it threaten labor costs or the continuity of production (i.e., the union agreement may be expiring)?

Finally, what are the overhead costs (such as rent, utilities, supervisory personnel, benefits, and the like)? You should check contracts, leases, and union agreements.

Taken together, how much of each sales dollar do these costs consume? In many manufacturing industries, a gross profit margin in the 20 to 30 percent range is reasonable; in retailing 30 to 40 percent is more typical (because sales volumes and asset turnover are greater).

Are there ways you—the buyer—could reduce costs and raise gross profits? Watch for opportunities to raise productivity by introducing new technologies, practices, plant, or equipment.

Do you see opportunities to reduce operating expenses? For example, general and administrative costs often are distorted in small, privately held companies. Could you reduce rental costs by infusing enough capital to buy plant or equipment? Keep in mind the fact that by replacing rental cost with depreciation (and, perhaps, interest expenses) you may not accomplish your goal. Could you reduce selling costs (advertising, commissions, and the like) by adopting new selling practices? By instituting preventive maintenance programs, could you increase the life expectancy of plant and machinery?

What are the candidate's interest expenses? Could you—by infusing capital—reduce debt and therefore lower this cost?

Your painstaking analysis of the candidate's costs may reveal opportunities for realizing savings that the present owner either overlooked or lacked the resources to develop.

One way to gauge the profitability of a candidate is to estimate its vulnerability to changes in the broader economy. This is done by estimating the company's *operating risk* and *financial risk.* Operating risk is the sensitivity of earnings to sudden changes in sales. It is greater when there is a larger proportion of fixed to variable costs. Financial risk is the sensitivity of earnings to the amount of debt in the capital structure. It is greater when there is greater debt or financial leverage. Companies with more debt tend to have more volatile earnings, all other things being equal.

BALANCE SHEET ANALYSIS   This task provides a check on the validity of reported earnings. If assets are overstated, or liabilities understated, then earnings will be overstated. You should look at the quality of reported assets and, if assets are overstated, adjust earnings to arrive at a more realistic figure.

Basically, the *quality* of an asset depends on its potential to generate profit, the timing of that profit and the risk that profit will not occur.

The greater the risk an asset possesses, the lower its quality. Assets are probable future economic benefits.

In judging the risk of realizing an asset, consider the effect of changing government policies on the value of that asset. For instance, because of a government ban on cyclamates, inventories of some foods and soft drinks had to be written off as unsalable. Likewise, bans on certain chemical agents have rendered inventories of pesticides worthless. Figure 4–2 shows risk levels associated with common assets. Figure 4–3 on page 66 shows several risk analysis techniques for assets.

Let's look at each type of asset in more detail:

CASH Note whether there are restricted cash balances. Cash held as a compensating balance or otherwise restricted and all monetary assets (cash and investments) held in foreign currency should also be noted.

ACCOUNTS RECEIVABLE Receivables are a key asset. They can be used as collateral or sold for cash.

Receivables due from other companies usually are safer than those due from retail consumers. The seller should give you an aging report of all receivables, indicating the terms of each one. If there are many old or unreliable receivables, you may have to adjust the balance sheet to reflect receivables that you believe are uncollectable. Is there a system for counting and evaluating inventory frequently? What about the ratio of current provision for doubtful accounts (write-offs) in relation to past provisions? Look especially for high-risk receivables such as those listed below:

- Amounts due from politically and economically unstable foreign governments or companies in such environments (these payments could be jeopardized as a result of nationalization, expropriation, confiscation, currency inconvertibility, trade embargos, and the like)
- Notes receivable involving an extension of credit given delinquent customers
- Amounts subject to right-of-return provisions
- Receivables originating from related parties
- A high proportion of receivables from a few customers

INVENTORY The ultimate objective in the evaluation of inventory is to determine if the inventory is consistently stated. Begin with a detailed list in which each item is classified by product, type, and age (raw material, work-in-process, or finished goods). Using the company's inventory records,

Figure 4–2. Major Types of Assets and Associated Risk Levels

Type of Asset	Risk Levels
1. Cash on hand at closing	Virtually None
2. Receivables from trade customers	Low
3. Receivable from a company in a problem industry	High
4. Work-in-process	High
5. Finished goods	Low
6. Investment portfolio of development companies	High
7. Diversified investment portfolio	Low
8. Land	Low
9. Specialized machinery for a "fad" product	High

inspect the inventory directly to assure yourself of its usability. Compare turnover in inventory with earlier years and other firms in the same industry.

Standard cost systems of large corporations might burden inventory with excessive overhead, resulting in excessive book values of inventory. Determine if this burden is reasonable.

As noted earlier in this chapter, the accounting method used in inventory dramatically affects its calculated value. This is especially true in times of high inflation. Where the FIFO method is used, the balance sheet more accurately reflects the current cost of the inventory, though income is overstated. Conversely, in the LIFO method, inventory value will usually be understated. Such an understated inventory may be "written up" after a purchase, to qualify for financing if you can prove its current value.

Other inventory items to watch for are purchase commitments, inventory held on consignment or consigned to others for sale, and if the company is involved in long-term contracts, the adequacy of accounting methods and their impact on inventory values.

PREPAID EXPENSES   Watch for any significant increase in prepaid expenses between years.

INVESTMENTS   Watch for frequent reclassifications (current asset to noncurrent asset and the reverse). Also, a declining trend in the percentage of earnings derived from investments to their carrying value may reveal increasing risk. Look at marketable securities, nonlisted securities, and equity investments.

PROPERTY, PLANT, AND EQUIPMENT   Focus on the degree of technological obsolescence of the equipment. After a review of a detailed list of all machinery, you should personally inspect major assets. After the tour, talk to manufacturers and appraisers to determine the market value of the equipment and the prospects for more productive replacements. You can use this to estimate future capital expenditures. Buildings and land may have appreciated and their value understated on the balance sheet. Check all leases. Remember that general-purpose buildings are easier to sell and often more valuable than cumbersome, single-purpose facilities.

ACCUMULATED DEPRECIATION   This is a contra-asset account. Compare the company's depreciation practices with industry norms. Watch for declining depreciation as a percentage of fixed assets. Also watch for changes in depreciation practices.

GOODWILL This is an intangible asset, but don't ignore it when it comes time to negotiate the purchase price. Goodwill is defined as the excess of purchase price over the fair market value of the net assets acquired. Because goodwill reduces earnings and is not deductible for tax purposes, it is critical to determine how much (if any) goodwill will be created as a result of your proposed acquisition.

You should then move to the other side of the balance sheet, making sure you've checked out all the major liabilities.

ACCOUNTS PAYABLE Begin by identifying trade creditors and other nonrecurring creditors. Note how long key suppliers have been in business, whether any alternate suppliers are available, and any special terms. Such terms may not transfer, and key suppliers may halt shipments when parties change. Trade creditors are quite sensitive to a change in company ownership, especially if the purchaser is highly leveraged.

To establish and maintain good relations with key suppliers, meet with them to build confidence. As noted earlier, the seller should provide you with a detailed current aging list of all trade payables. Calculate the ratio of purchases to trade payables for the last several months and years. If trade debt is already extended, find out if any creditors have filed or plan to file lawsuits to collect.

NOTES PAYABLE The seller should give you a detailed list of all notes payable by the company. This list should include the party to whom each note is payable, its date, original amount, current balance, interest rate, periodic payment, due dates, collateral, and any other terms. Watch for restrictive clauses or covenants that could affect the flexibility of future financing.

LONG-TERM DEBT As with short-term notes, the seller should give you a detailed list of all long-term debts, their conditions, restrictions, and payment schedules, and whether they are assumable if the debt is low cost.

Finally, review the net assets section of the balance sheet.

SHAREHOLDER'S EQUITY Look at the division of ownership of the stock of the company and the respective restrictions and rights of each shareholder class. Voting rights are important to consider because blocks of minority shareholders may attempt to prevent the sale. There are other important rights as well—dividend rights, redemption rights, retirement rights, and others.

If employees have a stock option or other benefit plan, you may not be legally required to continue it. However, morale of employees may be affected.

Figure 4–3. Risks and Analysis Techniques Associated with the Study of Assets

1. Low Quality Assets

Risks	Risk Analysis Techniques
• Asset valuations that are vulnerable to changes in economic, political, industrial, or corporate conditions	• Determine the turnover rates for each appropriate asset category.
• Cash assets having high realization risk	• Identify and classify assets according to their degree of risk and quantify the dollar exposure on high risk items.
• Suspicious deferral of costs	• Prepare ratios involving high risk assets. —Intangible assets plus deferred charges to total assets.
• Single-purpose assets	
• Assets vulnerable to changing government policies	
• Assets lacking separable value	
• Assets relating to the development and marketing of a risky new product	

2. Unavailability of Cash

Risks	Risk Analysis Techniques
• Cash that is restricted or not available	• Determine the amount of compensating balances.
• Poor cash management policies	• Determine the amount of cash being held by unfriendly foreign governments.
	• Compute for several years the ratios of (1) sales to cash, (2) net income to cash, and (3) cash to total current assets.

3. Overstated Receivables

Risks	Risk Analysis Techniques
• Receivables that may not be realized	• Identify and determine the dollar amount of risky receivables.
• Sudden write-offs of accounts	• Calculate and analyze accounts receivable turnover, the number of days accounts receivable are held, and the ratios of accounts receivable to total assets, and accounts receivable to sales.
• A high percentage of receivables from individuals rather than corporations	• Look at ratings given by credit agencies (such as Dun & Bradstreet) for the candidate's customers.
• Factoring of accounts receivable	

RATIO ANALYSIS Ratio analysis helps point out trends that could be good or bad for you, the new owner. Ratios spotlight strengths and weaknesses. After arriving at our own adjusted versions of the candidate's income statement and balance sheet, you can calculate several simple ratios. Usually you compare the candidate's ratios to those of other companies in the same industry. Three of the more common ratios are described below.

CURRENT AND QUICK RATIOS A measure of liquidity and ability to meet current obligations.

$$\text{Current Ratio} = \frac{\text{Current Assets}}{\text{Current Liabilities}}$$

$$\text{Quick Ratio} = \frac{\text{Cash} + \text{Net Accounts Receivable}}{\text{Current Liabilities}}$$

The quick ratio is a purer measure of liquidity than the current ratio as it excludes inventory, which might have to be sold at a discount. A current ratio greater than 3:1 and a quick ratio greater than 1.5:1 for instance, are generally considered high for a manufacturing company. Companies with such high ratios are "cash-rich" because liquid assets have not been invested in long-term assets like plant and equipment. Such companies are often sought for mergers, so that a "cash-poor" company can employ the cash. These ratios are more useful in industrial companies than in financial and other service companies.

DEBT TO EQUITY RATIO This ratio is a measure of the company's strain in its borrowing capacity.

$$\text{Debt/Equity Ratio} = \frac{\text{Long-Term Liabilities}}{\text{Common and Preferred Stockholders' Equity}}$$

Depending on the industry, analysts may consider a ratio greater than 1:1 as a mild danger and a ratio greater than 2:1—which means twice as much borrowing as shareholders' equity in the corporation—as a very strong danger signal. A company with a low ratio might become the target of a company with a high ratio; the latter, by acquiring it, would pick up substantial borrowing capacity—much like acquiring an unused line of credit. This of course, would be dependent on how much the buyer financed the purchase of the target.

In analyzing a target company, it is important to track trends in financial performance. Table 4–1 lists some of the financial ratios typically used to analyze a hypothetical company. This exhibit lists the balance sheet, income statement, financial ratio calculations, and ratio definitions of a typical manufacturing company.

TABLE 4-1(a)
Balance Sheet for KSS Manufacturing Company

	1976	1977	1978	1979	1980	1981	1982	1983	1984	1985
ASSETS:										
CURRENT ASSETS:										
Cash	2,368	2,307	2,351	2,383	2,421	2,467	2,521	2,582	2,649	2,724
Accounts Receivable	8,811	8,917	9,054	9,327	9,684	10,502	10,886	11,764	11,894	12,007
Inventories	11,207	11,889	12,507	12,986	13,542	14,056	14,898	15,672	16,205	17,286
Prepaid Expense/Other	502	553	588	605	654	711	749	886	943	1,043
TOTAL CURRENT ASSETS	22,888	23,666	24,500	25,301	26,301	27,736	29,054	30,904	31,691	33,060
LONG-TERM ASSETS:										
Property, Plant, & Equipment	20,120	18,605	17,279	16,119	15,104	14,216	13,439	12,759	12,164	11,644
Investments	2,010	4,892	6,727	9,507	12,862	16,708	21,045	25,885	31,245	37,145
Other Assets	2,893	2,812	2,857	2,888	2,927	2,975	3,034	3,102	3,178	3,263
TOTAL LONG-TERM ASSETS	25,023	26,309	26,863	28,514	30,893	33,899	37,518	41,746	46,587	52,052
TOTAL ASSETS	47,911	49,975	51,363	53,815	57,194	61,635	66,572	72,650	78,278	85,112
LIABILITIES AND SHAREHOLDERS' INVESTMENT:										
CURRENT LIABILITIES:										
Current Maturities	617	1,982	1,686	1,449	1,259	1,107	986	889	811	749
Accounts Payable	3,927	4,002	4,264	4,558	4,730	4,992	5,008	5,257	5,616	5,891
Accrued Expenses	1,947	2,012	2,078	2,200	2,312	2,387	2,417	2,509	2,654	2,718
Income Taxes Current	1,183	1,267	1,388	1,502	1,794	1,888	1,907	2,024	2,218	2,488
TOTAL CURRENT LIABILITIES	7,674	9,263	9,416	9,709	10,095	10,374	10,318	10,679	11,299	11,846
LONG-TERM LIABILITIES:										
Long-Term Indebtedness	9,411	7,928	6,743	5,794	5,035	4,428	3,943	3,554	3,243	2,995
Other	551	570	522	486	447	406	362	317	269	219
TOTAL LONG-TERM LIABILITIES	9,962	8,498	7,265	6,280	5,482	4,834	4,305	3,871	3,512	3,214
SHAREHOLDERS' INVESTMENT	30,275	32,214	34,682	37,826	41,617	46,427	51,949	58,100	63,467	70,052
TOTAL LIAB. + SHR. INVESTMENT	47,911	49,975	51,363	53,815	57,194	61,635	66,572	72,650	78,278	85,112

TABLE 4-1(b)
Income Statement for KSS Manufacturing Company ($000)

	1976	1977	1978	1979	1980	1981	1982	1983	1984	1985
REVENUES:										
Tractor/Trailer Division	66,213	68,632	73,224	76,595	79,961	83,479	87,156	90,992	94,994	99,173
Heavy Equipment Division	33,422	30,701	32,113	33,592	35,068	36,610	38,223	39,905	41,660	43,493
TOTAL REVENUES	99,635	99,333	105,337	110,187	115,029	120,089	125,379	130,897	136,654	142,666
COSTS AND EXPENSES:										
Cost of Goods Sold	80,357	80,297	85,181	89,104	93,019	97,111	101,389	105,851	110,506	115,369
G&A/Selling/Other	6,972	6,891	7,272	7,607	7,941	8,290	8,656	9,037	9,434	9,849
Depreciation	2,760	2,515	2,326	2,160	2,015	1,888	1,777	1,680	1,595	1,521
Interest Expense	293	1,015	1,029	957	831	729	649	584	532	491
Interest Income	(62)	(77)	(759)	(1,098)	(1,515)	(2,018)	(2,595)	(3,246)	(3,972)	(4,776)
TOTAL COSTS & EXPENSES	90,320	90,641	95,049	98,730	102,291	106,000	109,876	113,906	118,095	122,454
INCOME BEFORE TAX	9,315	8,692	10,288	11,457	12,738	14,089	15,503	16,991	18,559	20,212
INCOME TAXES	4,409	4,114	4,869	5,423	6,029	6,668	7,338	8,042	8,784	9,566
NET INCOME	4,906	4,578	5,419	6,034	6,709	7,421	8,165	8,949	9,775	10,646

TABLE 4–1(c)
Ratio Analysis for KSS Manufacturing Company

	1976	1977	1978	1979	1980	1981	1982	1983	1984	1985
LIQUIDITY RATIOS:										
Current Ratio	2.98	2.55	2.60	2.61	2.61	2.67	2.82	2.89	2.80	2.79
Acid Test	1.46	1.21	1.21	1.21	1.20	1.25	1.30	1.34	1.29	1.24
LEVERAGE RATIOS:										
Debt to Equity	0.58	0.55	0.48	0.42	0.37	0.33	0.28	0.25	0.23	0.21
L/T Debt to Equity	0.33	0.26	0.21	0.17	0.13	0.10	0.08	0.07	0.06	0.05
Times Interest Earned	31.79	8.56	10.00	11.97	15.33	19.33	23.89	29.09	34.89	41.16
Debt to Capital Employed	0.25	0.21	0.17	0.14	0.12	0.09	0.08	0.06	0.05	0.04
ACTIVITY RATIOS:										
Inventory Turnover	6.58	6.95	6.98	6.99	7.01	7.04	7.00	6.93	6.93	6.89
Average Daily Revenue	276.76	275.93	292.60	306.08	319.53	333.58	348.28	363.60	379.59	396.29
Average Collection Period	31.84	32.32	30.94	30.47	30.31	31.48	31.26	32.35	31.33	30.30
PROFITABILITY RATIOS:										
Return on Capital Employed (ROI)	0.12	0.11	0.13	0.14	0.14	0.14	0.15	0.14	0.16	0.15
Return on Total Assets	0.19	0.17	0.20	0.21	0.22	0.23	0.23	0.23	0.24	0.24
Return on Equity Capital	0.30	0.28	0.31	0.32	0.32	0.32	0.32	0.31	0.31	0.30
Gross Margin Ratio	0.19	0.19	0.19	0.19	0.19	0.19	0.19	0.19	0.19	0.19
Net Income on Revenue	0.05	0.05	0.05	0.05	0.06	0.06	0.07	0.07	0.07	0.07

TABLE 4-1(d)
Financial Ratio Analysis for KSS Manufacturing Company

RATIO FORMULAS

Liquidity Ratios:

1. Current Ratio (same as Working Capital Ratio): Total current assets divided by total current liabilities.
2. Acid Test: Cash and cash equivalents plus net accounts receivable (accounts receivable less allowances) divided by total current liabilities.

Leverage Ratios:

3. Debt to Equity: Total current liabilities plus long-term debt divided by shareholders' equity.
4. Long-Term Debt to Equity: Long-term debt divided by shareholders' equity.
5. Times Interest Earned: Income before tax divided by interest expense.
6. Debt to Capital Employed: Long-term debt divided by the sum of long-term debt and shareholders' equity.

Activity Ratios:

7. Inventory Turnover: Cost of goods sold divided by the average of opening and closing inventory.
8. Average Daily Sales: Net sales divided by 360.
9. Average Collection Period: Net accounts receivable (accounts receivable less allowances) divided by average daily sales.

Profitability Ratios:

10. Return on Total Capital Employed (ROI): Net income after tax divided by the sum of long-term debt and shareholders' equity.
11. Return on Total Assets: Income before tax divided by total assets.
12. Return on Equity Capital: Income before tax divided by average shareholders' equity.
13. Gross Margin Ratio: Net sales minus cost of goods sold divided by net sales.
14. Net Income on Sales: Net income (income after taxes) divided by net sales.

4.4 OPERATIONAL ASSESSMENT

While you should begin the operations review with an objective attitude, it may pay to be a little skeptical. The main purpose of the review is to uncover inefficiency and opportunity in the day-to-day operations of the candidate. Just as you should be skeptical about accounting practices during the financial assessment, you should be skeptical about plant, equipment, and methods during this review of operations. Study the controls and look for ways to improve.

- **Property, Plant, and Equipment.** Are the buildings and machines up to date? Could you utilize them more fully? Why are the plants located where they are—access to markets, materials, transportation, or personnel? Watch for hidden value in real property—could you sublet or sell the property more profitably?
- **Production Controls.** What controls does management exercise over manufacturing operations? Production, inventory, and quality controls are critical.
- **Purchasing.** Purchasing is important and relatively straight forward. Study the candidate's major suppliers, especially single-source suppliers. Are they financially sound and dependable for quality and delivery?
- **Research and Development.** R & D should be a technological divining rod, warning of the passing old and the emerging new methods, materials, and systems. From the candidate's research spending, personnel, and facilities you may infer the level and flavor of management's commitment to progress.

A full, overall checklist for your analysis of finance, operations, and other areas appears at the end of this chapter.

4.5 MARKETING ANALYSIS

Your analysis of the candidate's marketing activities is arguably the most important part of Level III screening. Solid finances, efficient operations, and hard-working people are not enough if the candidate cannot compete, sell, and deliver in the marketplace. Six major marketing areas are described. For each area, try to uncover management information in support of your assessment.

- **Products and Services.** Are the product lines cohesive? How do they compare with those of the competition for features, quality, price, reputation, service? (Which of these is most important to buyers?) Note any gaps or redundancies in the product line. Are the products technologically up to date?

- **Marketing Plan.** What is the underlying marketing strategy? Has it changed in recent years? Note major features of the strategy—terms and credit policies, incentives, and discounts.

- **Pricing.** How important is price in this market (compared to features, service, quality, and other selling points)? How does the candidate's price structure compare with that of the competition? Watch for significantly high or low pricing—a sign of danger. Also watch for odd trends in pricing over the last few years.

- **Channels of Distribution.** Does the channel deliver "the right product to the right marketplace," the right buyers? Look for ways to cut costs by introducing automation, vertical integration, and new channels.

- **Market.** Who are the candidates' major customers? Watch for trends. Could you move into new markets easily? What proportion of sales are to the government, the military, or to wholesalers? What's the resale market? How much turnover is there in the market?

- **Marketing Organization.** How are marketing personnel organized, deployed, managed, compensated? How is information from the field and other marketing research handled? Advertising and other tools?

4.6 ASSESSMENT OF MANAGEMENT AND PERSONNEL

The critical task here is simple to state, but subtle and complex to analyze: integration. Will the candidate's organization be absorbed into your own, or be left alone? What would the resulting organization look like? Watch for opportunities to cut costs by excising redundant functions.

But by far most important, how will the merger or acquisition be received by the candidate's management and employees? This is difficult to study (because you must study an intangible reaction to a hypothetical event, usually in secrecy). Major risks include the loss or demoralization of key personnel, disputes with organized labor, "overwhelming" the acquired company, and overextending the management of your own company. You'll need more than an ounce of prevention to overcome these risks. More will be said about risks and strategies in Chapter 6.

For now, do your homework. Be careful not to draw undue attention to your review in this area, as you may unnecessarily anger or alarm management and employees of the candidate. You should study the organization on the following points:

- **Entrepreneurship.** Are managers alert, competitive, progressive? Are there signs of innovation and involvement?
- **Coordination.** Is the company clearly and firmly structured? Watch for managers and other leaders who could introduce, coordinate, and help manage the transition.
- **Attitudes.** Watch for signs of conflict between management and labor, between divisions, between key managers. Are people committed to the overall success of the company? Study previous practices in appraisal and compensation. Look at turnover.
- **Management.** What are the educational and work backgrounds of key managers? Have incentive and development programs been established, and are they effective? Do you see signs of motivation? Of disinterest?
- **Work Force.** Note the rates of absenteeism, turnover, productivity, promotion. Are there managers who come from the work force? What training programs are available?

How should you study the management and personnel of a candidate? Even if the merger or acquisition is not occurring under hostile circumstances, the seller may require that you work in secrecy. However, do not risk the entire purchase by misrepresenting yourself to those you contact. As circumstances permit, observe managers and employees in the workplace. Interview officers and, when possible, key employees who can voice the attitudes of labor. Hunt for power brokers and opinion leaders and get to know them.

4.7 PUTTING IT ALL TOGETHER

To help you tie together everything you've learned, this section offers a tool developed by Touche Ross & Co. Figure 4–4 is a checklist to help you make sure you've covered everything. It includes important points concerning the proposed acquisition—a business summary, as well as marketing, manufacturing, management, and financial information. It is important to remember that this is a generalized checklist, and that different items may also be analyzed and emphasized, depending on the target under consideration. The expertise of the people conducting the review is critical to its success.

Figure 4-4. Touche Ross & Co. Acquisition Review

1. **Transaction Summary**

   - Business reasons for acquiring
   - Seller's objectives
   - Asking price
   - Valuation of target
   - Rationale for premium/discount
   - Pro forma shareholder dilution
   - Financial structure of transaction
   - Accounting and tax treatment
   - Letter of intent

2. **Company Background Information**

   - General description of the company's development
   - Date and location of incorporation
   - Founding shareholders and directors
   - Existing ownership (names and percent of holdings)
   - Company's major developments/achievements to date
   - Name of professional service providers (accountants, lawyers, investment bankers)
   - History of acquisitions

3. **Business Summary**

   - Description of major product lines and services
   - Distribution of sales by market segment
   - List of primary customers (greater than 10 percent of gross sales)
   - Breakdown of sales by industries and domestic vs. foreign
   - List of primary suppliers (greater than 10 percent of purchases)
   - Product brand names, price ranges, and quality
   - Description of patents, trademarks, and other barriers to competitive entry
   - Description of regulatory or technical trends that might be favorable or unfavorable to the company
   - List of significant long-term contracts (labor, supply, or sales)

Figure 4–4. Touche Ross & Co. Acquisition Review (cont'd)

4. Marketing, Sales, and Distribution

- General description of the company's sales and distribution methods
- Description of the market, history, size, trend, and company's position in the market
- Description of the end users
- Sales of the company and industry for the last five years and for the expected next five years
- Number of customers in active accounts (list by volume in descending order)
- Description of important factors of the company's sales policy (such as price, quality, service, etc.). Why does the customer buy the product?
- Description of franchise terms, if any
- Detail on the importance of foreign competition
- Description of any special relationship with customers
- Detailed description of channels of distribution
- Description of the sales organization (compensation method, management abilities, cost per sales dollar, etc.)
- Advertising—cost and assessment of effectiveness
- Pricing policies—description for each product line and comparison with industry standards
- Description of how the company's products are moved to the customers
- Description of research and development programs

5. Manufacturing

- Description of all facilities (location, square feet, age, condition, number of floors, appraised value, etc.)
- Capacity of each facility and utilization
- List major pieces of equipment (condition, location, appraised value, etc.)
- Assess each facility's layout, production controls, shipping and receiving controls
- Detail the conditions and terms of any leases
- Explain the rationale for each facility's location
- Description of future capital expenditures (planned or needed)
- Level of outside subcontracting
- Description of maintenance programs

6. Management and Work Force

- Organization chart detailing department heads and number of people
- Description of management—experience, position, age, compensation, etc.

Figure 4–4. Touche Ross & Co. Acquisition Review (cont'd)

- Description of work force—number, skilled/unskilled, union/nonunion, strike record, morale, full time/part time, etc.
- Comparison of company to industry standards—compensation, revenues per employee, fringe benefits, etc.
- Rate of turnover for each personnel level (explanation if turnover is very high or low)
- List terms of union contracts
- Pension fund liabilities—funded or unfunded
- Detailed description of key officers—family relationships, investment in company, intention to continue after the acquisition, apparent skill, amount of time devoted to business

7. Competition

- Description of all major competitors—sales, earnings, market share, strengths, and weaknesses
- Nature of trade practices
- Barriers to new competitive entry
- Comparison of pricing vs. the competition
- Description of value, packaging, and utility comparisons
- Effects of regulatory agencies on competition

8. Financial

- Audited annual reports (last 5–10 years)
- Yearly projection of balance sheet, income statement, and cash flow (next 5 years)
- Trend ratio analysis (liquidity, leverage, activity, and profitability)
- Analysis of appropriateness of accounting procedures and methods
- Analysis of variances
- Descriptions and analysis of all balance sheet and income statement accounts
- Tax returns (last 5 years)
- Aging of accounts receivable
- Description of any hidden assets
- Discussion of company's profit plan

9. Capitalization

- Equity (common and preferred)
  - —Total shares authorized and outstanding
  - —Description of covenants and terms

Figure 4-4. Touche Ross & Co. Acquisition Review (cont'd)

—List of major shareholders and their holdings

—Description of trading activity

• Debt

—List lenders and contact personnel (banks, insurance companies, etc.)

—Detail the agreements and restrictions for each long-term debt obligation (amount, term, collateral, etc.)

—Description of lines of credit

—Assessment of unused debt capacity

—Description of all short-term debt arrangements

—Description of contingent liabilities

Negotiating

5

5.1 INTRODUCTION

This chapter describes the negotiating process, which enables you to:

- Decide whether the acquisition should be made
- Determine the purchase price
- Develop the acquisition contract

The last item, the acquisition contract, starts out as an agreement in principle. This, in turn, is followed by an exhaustive investigation of the seller's business. A detailed acquisition contract is then prepared.

This chapter approaches the subject of acquisitions through friendly negotiations, where there is a willing seller. The implementation of a hostile tender offer or proxy battle to gain control of a company is quite different from the approach taken in a friendly acquisition. However, the basic negotiating principles described in this chapter are useful in any acquisition.

Information gathered throughout the negotiation process leads to the following decisions:

1. Terminate negotiations, or
2. Continue to hold discussions and seek additional information and, ultimately
3. Determine, based on reasonably complete information, what purchase price to offer.

5.2 PREPARING FOR THE NEGOTIATIONS

The key to most successful negotiations is adequate preparation. In fact, preparation is often more critical than strategy, even in the most complex of negotiations. You can reduce these complexities and avoid potential problems by carrying out comprehensive prenegotiation research and planning. Determine which negotiation factors the company values most highly. Find out who the other company's negotiators are, or who is likely to handle the transaction.

Negotiations are nothing more than a series of meetings between two teams—buyers and sellers. Both teams should comprise a continuity of enthusiastic personnel throughout the usually lengthy negotiation process. There are so many levels of necessary information, from financial data to the personalities of the negotiators, and the volume of information is often so large, that each side should make an exhaustive analysis of the other company and its representatives and present an equally complete picture of what they have to contribute. Each negotiating team should know what the other team is likely to offer or accept. How much cash do they have on hand? Can they make financial decisions on their own, or must they defer to their management? If we consent to A, are they likely to give us B? *Can* they give us B?

5.3 YOUR NEGOTIATING TEAM

The core of your negotiating team should be business executives with the authority to recommend that the acquisition take place and to approve a purchase price.

All your team members should be enthusiastic. But choose your senior negotiator with special care. This person should know the business, be a leader for your other negotiators, and be a formidable presence in the eyes of the other team.

It is the role of the chief executive to keep the negotiating team in balance. Too often the team becomes the advocate of the deal and not the company they represent. The urge to close is a powerful one. The first priority is to make sure the transaction still makes sense.

Once assembled, your negotiating team can begin researching the target company. A primary goal of such research is to discover how the company is doing in its respective markets. An indirect way of doing this is to look at the company's reputation in its industry. A company with a strong reputation is more likely to be negotiating from a position of strength than an unpopular company. Reputation is built on performance and policy, so look at both. Do they put all their eggs in one basket, or do they have several fields of interest? Compare the target company to its competitors. Is it a strong company? What is its pricing structure? Look for historical trends in the market data. Have they been losing money consistently? How are they doing this year compared with last?

Your negotiating team should perform a complete financial analysis of the other company. How much is it really worth? Are there hidden weaknesses in the financial data? Remember that many companies can be made to appear profitable, at least on the surface. It may take digging to spot the flaws in a financial record. You may find that the company is worth $5 million right now, but what will it be worth in five years if it continues to operate as it does now?

Learn all you can about the other company's management. Remember that its negotiating team may merely be carrying out the desires of a few top managers. What is the company's management history? A newly appointed CEO is not likely to behave the same way as a 40-year veteran nearing retirement. Study the management structure, as well as the personalities involved. How are decisions made? What is the chain of command? Although the chief negotiator may have the authority to close a deal, he or she may only be representing higher management. Find out this individual's standing in the eyes of the Board of Directors. Will the Board support a controversial concession? Or will the negotiator be second-guessed?

It is also important to find out how the other company's management feels about your company and your representatives. Have they ever had any dealings with your company or your negotiating team? If so, how did those negotiations turn out, and who was involved? Anticipate what they might have in store for you. Try to guess what their answers to some of your questions are likely to be, and plan your questions accordingly. Once you fully research the target company, you will have taken the critical first step toward preparing for negotiations.

5.4 ALLOCATING RESOURCES

When you have examined the target company's strengths, weaknesses, fears, and desires and compared them to those of your own company, decide where to concentrate most of your efforts. You should foresee a reasonably likely outcome of the negotiations and determine how to reach that outcome most efficiently. From the initial meeting to the close of the acquisition, volumes of information will be exchanged and studied; positions will be presented, retracted, and reinterpreted. Know your target before going for it and know how strong it is. And keep these points in mind:

- It is extremely important to both sides of a business negotiation to state precisely what is being bought.

- If you are buying a company in pieces, all the pieces may not be included in the agreement.

- You may be looking just for a controlling interest in shares, and may not wish to buy the company outright.

- You cannot afford to forgo an exhaustive analysis of the target company.

- An incomplete valuation may significantly affect the price to which you ultimately agree.

As you select the particular parts of a target company, also formulate an acquisition strategy. Besides clearly stating what you are buying and establishing a price range (which the seller, of course, will do as well), you should consider many variables. Here are five elements to keep in mind during the early stages of negotiations:

1. Contingent payments
2. Installment payments (over time)
3. Guaranteed payments
4. Payments in stock
5. Options

As the buyer, you can influence these the most (since only you can ultimately decide whether you can handle the payments). As you work toward a tentative offer, keep in mind the fact that cash down payments are generally less than 30 percent of the full price. The acquirer typically tries to maximize his or her return by using various financial instruments.

The price and structure of the deal will determine the funding needed to finance it. Identify your sources in advance. Once this backing is established, you may pursue a negotiating strategy.

5.5 ESTABLISHING STRATEGY

There are several points to remember when establishing a negotiating strategy:

- **Be prepared.** Planning means looking at your own company, the other company, and the markets in which the latter operates.
- **Be patient.** Negotiations seldom are completed quickly.
- **Be enthusiastic.** This enthusiasm should affect every member of your negotiating team.

Reflect a positive attitude throughout the negotiations. Know in advance what you must bring to the negotiations, how you will defend your various positions, and how you will handle the target company's reactions to you. Make a list of priorities in terms of what you can offer and what you'd like in return. You may want to use these common techniques:

1. Arrange for negotiations to take place at your location since you are likely to be most confident there.
2. Take the initiative by preparing a proposal before the other side does.
3. Make sure people on your negotiating team can speak persuasively.
4. At meetings, place your senior negotiator at the head of the table.
5. Project an image of confidence by being well-prepared and organized.

You must decide where and when to employ these strategies. Whether you use them or not, it is to your advantage as a negotiator to know them, to avoid being fooled yourself.

5.6 THE NEGOTIATIONS

Successful acquisitions require proper preparation. Too often a deal fails for reasons that could have been foreseen and avoided. A successful deal should satisfy both your needs and those of the seller.

Of course, it is not always easy to determine real needs—they should be viewed in the light of the acquisition at hand. Since every acquisition is different, each should be seen individually. The ultimate goal of negotiation is not to "squeeze" the best deal but to gain advantages for both sides. Of course, you will try for the most attractive deal from your point of view, but keep your reputation in mind when considering an agreement that favors you unfairly. You may later be involved with the target company on some other business matter—you may even own it—and the ill will may hurt you more in the long run. Negotiations should be carried out in a friendly, honest atmosphere since no one likes to feel uncomfortable. Treat your negotiating opponents as you prefer to be treated: with honesty, a sense of rapport, and optimism gilded with enthusiasm for the acquisition and the companies involved.

The best advice for a negotiator is to know the persons with whom you are negotiating and know the company you are seeking to acquire. That means not only considering the financial aspects of the business relationship, but also looking at the business synergy between the companies and the respective managements. Don't assume that the other company will try to cheat you, since this attitude may undermine your attitude. Here are guidelines for prospective buyers:

- Don't enter into negotiations unless you are reasonably sure that you want to buy.
- Hold detailed questions until later in the negotiations.
- Sell yourself at the first meeting, stressing your attitude of cooperation, reasonableness, and genuine interest in the seller.
- The seller should be equally familiar and comfortable with the person who will step in if you are not present.
- Bring up early anything you feel the seller may have forgotten. He or she may thank you later.
- Allay any fears the seller may have about the postmerger period.
- Enter negotiations with a ballpark figure on price and some notion of terms. Know your price limits, and make sure they're consistent with the realities of the marketplace.
- Respond to the seller's needs.
- Don't try too hard to get the best deal. Work toward what is fair.
- Think of the target company in terms of a synergistic relationship in the future.

Facts must always be verified, particularly when it comes to money. Don't procrastinate. Follow through as directly as you can without being hasty. Of course, this is a fine line, but you should get to the point where you are sure of something and then say so.

There are three elements in the negotiating process: power, timing, and information. Each of these comprises several variables.

POWER   Look at the power of a negotiating team as the sum of four variables:

1. **Resource commitment.** The amount of money and/or time spent on the negotiations varies directly with a negotiator's willingness to compromise.
2. **Alternatives.** The more negotiating alternatives you have, the better your position. Be sure to set priorities on your options.
3. **Experience.** Be well-prepared and possess the proper background. The other company's team should know that you have these credentials.
4. **Knowledge of the other negotiator.** The more you know about what is important to the opposing negotiators, the better you can anticipate how they will react to your actions.

TIMING   Business deals always are undertaken with respect to some schedule or another. Be aware of your own deadlines, and try to discover theirs. Try to maintain an accelerating pace throughout the negotiations. A lull in the activity could give the seller cold feet.

INFORMATION   Again, "know thyself" and know with whom you are dealing. Preparation is the key.

Through the negotiations, you are attempting to reach three conclusions:

1. Should you buy the other company?
2. What price should you pay?
3. What kind of contract terms do you want?

The further you've gone with the acquisition process and the closer you are to reaching an agreement, the more the time and expense required. As an acquisition draws closer to conclusion, price often becomes the main concern and options may be offered to compensate when the seller's price is too high. Once a price is agreed upon, many activities in the negotiating process will be carried out by each company's attorneys. At this point your accounting firm or advisor should be asked to conduct a business review of the target company. Your attorney should draft the contracts, help you to examine all the legal details, and prepare any necessary registration statements and prospectuses. Tax aspects of the transaction and the accounting treatment are especially important. While the detailed contract is being negotiated, your accountant or financial advisor may supply you with additional information (beyond the acquisition audit) about the target company's financial statements and its tangible and intangible assets.

When major features of a deal have nearly been resolved, issues involving management salaries and bonuses may become important. This is because the other side sees an agreement close at hand, and feels that it has an opportunity to sweeten the pot. This is also when you must draw the line on contingent liability. Assuming that the acquisition takes place, what would happen if your business folded next year? And what if that failure were caused by the acquired company? Be sure to secure a right of inspection prior to the closing and a right to terminate the acquisition without liability under certain circumstances. Finally, good timing for payment can make the most tedious of negotiations well worth the effort.

The most obvious way of concluding an acquisition is for you to turn over cash, notes, voting stock, or other assets to the seller. But this process often is complex, especially if the seller remains at the helm.

There are several methods you may follow to arrive at an arrangement where the selling price is determined by contingent earnings. The contingent earnout bridges the gap between your offer and the seller's asking price. This gap may exist because the seller has depressed earnings to save on taxes or may be the result of differences in opinion on the earning potential of the seller. One approach to this situation would be to increase your offer by adding one or more contingency payments if future earnings warrant them.

Contingent payout is a powerful concept from two perspectives. First, it helps the acquirer do the deal by allowing them to pay less for the company upfront and thereby lessening the risk of the transaction. Second, this deal structure provides a strong incentive to the seller to make the company succeed after the transaction closes. It is, however, important to structure these transactions very carefully and account for such items as overhead allocations from the parent.

There are many ways to structure a contingent payment provision. Two common methods are average earnout and percentage of profit earnout.

- **Average earnout.** In this approach, you and the seller agree on what you expect future earnings of the acquired company to be. If these earnings are realized, the seller gets his or her asking price. If they are not, no further payment is made.

- **Percentage of profit earnout.** Under this arrangement, you pay the seller a fixed sum at closing and an earnout percentage paid either annually or at the end of a specified period.

Earnouts are most appropriate in acquisitions where some separation of business functions continues after the merger. It may not be possible to accomplish this if the facilities and resources of the seller become so closely meshed with yours that it proves difficult to sort out which of you is responsible for future earnings.

One last thing to consider when thinking about price in an acquisition is goodwill, which is the excess of purchase price over book value. Goodwill will have to be written off in the years to come and will reduce earnings but is not deductible for tax purposes. Only you can decide what you want, how much you are willing to pay for it, and what risks you are willing to take. A good business deal is one in which you give the other party good reason to be confident that the deal is a wise one. But you must convince yourself first.

Chapter 6 describes valuation—a process that is closely related to negotiation. In fact, the amount to be paid is typically the most important negotiation issue.

Setting the Price

6

6.1 INTRODUCTION

This chapter discusses valuation, the process used to develop a supportable opinion on the worth of a business. There are many reasons for performing this appraisal, some not so obvious. Of course, valuation often is the first step in the purchase or sale of a business. Here are other instances where a business appraisal comes into play.

1. Shareholder buy-sell agreements
2. Recapitalization
3. Strategic planning (resource allocation between business segments)
4. Litigation
5. Employee stock ownership plans
6. Tax calculation support (with regard, for instance, to gifts and contributions)
7. Estate planning
8. Management incentive plans
9. Required distributions by private foundations

A detailed explanation of valuation methods is beyond the scope of this book. Instead, this chapter will acquaint you with valuation in general and with some common techniques. In particular, this chapter describes procedures used to establish the value of a business for acquisition purposes.

In buy-sell agreements, the owners of a closely held company frequently plan for possible transfers of stock among shareholders. Such agreements may provide a formula for valuation to set a price, such as a multiple of book value or of earnings. Alternatively, the price may be open and require the parties to arrive at a value. You can best achieve a fair price if you and the target company's representatives are experienced in the analysis of financial data and in the interpretation of financial theory.

The assets of an established business will often be purchased for a set price without determining the dollar value of its components. It becomes necessary to assign values to these components for purposes of depreciation, amortization, tax planning, and accounting. A professional appraisal after the transaction closes is often made in such situations to protect the buyer against the tax collector's allocation of excessive amounts to goodwill.

There are many valid reasons why a particular business may have different values to different parties. The purpose of the valuation will frequently affect the technique used and the value developed. The taxable value of a business for estate tax purposes, for instance, while theoretically representing fair market value, may in fact be quite different from the price it would command on the open market. Generally, valuations entail an opinion (in monetary terms) of the future benefits the business can provide. You are usually seeking a monetary return on your investment and of your time. The proposed acquisition represents only one of many ways in which your money could be invested.

Risk must be taken into consideration when you calculate the value of the firm. Risk is usually reflected in the assumed cost of capital, the expected rate of return you would require to induce you to purchase the business. One acquirer may apply a higher cost of capital, resulting in a lower valuation and therefore a lower price, because he or she perceives a higher degree of risk. Another acquirer with greater confidence in the company may evaluate it on the basis of a lower cost of capital. As the cost of capital goes up, the present value of a given stream of future expected dollars goes down, and vice versa.

Although "value" means different things to accountants, economists, business-people, lawyers, and tax agents, the term does have a distinguishing characteristic. "All values are anticipations of the future" was how Oliver Wendell Holmes said it. Value depends on your perception of the usefulness of the item under question. Whether a price is too high or low depends upon the expected results of the business, which can never be predicted with certainty. The validity of any price conclusions rests upon forecasts and assumptions of what may occur in the future.

Valuation provides a base from which to reach the acquisition price. Valuation provides a range of figures by gauging the *future* value of a business. These numbers may be based on a cash flow projection or other methods that incorporate future performance expectations and are at best a guess, but they should be an educated guess. Value is a calculated figure of the worth of a company, whereas the ultimate price paid for the company is a figure negotiated between a willing buyer and seller. Companies are generally appraised according to one or more of the following techniques (see Section 6.2 for a more detailed explanation of valuation techniques):

1. **Discounted cash flow.** This method requires a forecast of cash flow for some time into the future. Preparing a reliable forecast is one of the most complex features of the discounted cash flow analysis. The forecast should take into account the company's historical financial performance, the need for future financial capital expenditures, the interrelationships between income statement and balance sheet line items and should incorporate growth expectations for the company's industry and market area. The present value of this cash flow is then computed. Any value of the assets of the business expected to remain at the end of the cash flow period is then valued on a discounted basis (terminal value). The value of the company is the discounted value of the cash flows plus the present worth of the residual assets less any liabilities expected to remain.

2. **Comparable transaction analysis.** With this analysis you create a pricing benchmark by seeing what other similar companies were sold for, and then use that benchmark to imput a value on your target company. The difficulty with this analysis is finding other transactions which can be deemed comparable to your proposed transaction.

3. **Comparable company analysis.** The idea here is to look at comparable P/Es for similar companies (the hard part is finding appropriate comparables and weighing their market price against that of the company you're valuing). It is easier in the case of public companies, where P/Es are readily available. These P/Es should be compared to the historical performance of industry standards (see Chapter 2 for industry data sources).

4. **Asset analysis.** Fixed asset value equals the cost of building the facility from scratch, less physical deterioration and functional obsolescence of each major asset. Market demand for a particular asset will also affect its value. Depreciation, use by the buyer, and other factors are built into the value of fixed assets. Besides fixed assets, you also should consider the target company's cash on hand, marketable securities, accounts receivable, and inventory. Be sure that what is on paper adequately reflects the real situation.

5. **Payback theory.** Payback theory asks how long it will take you to get back your investment from the target company.

These four techniques are discussed in detail in the next section. Many factors must be considered in a valuation:

1. The nature of the business and its history
2. The economic outlook in general and that of the industry in particular
3. The book value of the company's stock and the financial condition of the business
4. The company's earning capacity
5. The company's dividend-paying capacity
6. The goodwill and other intangible value of the company
7. Prior sales of the company's stock and the size of the block to be sold
8. Comparisons with companies in similar lines of business whose stocks are actively traded in open markets

The theoretical definition of "risk" requires an understanding of basic statistics since it involves the use of variance or standard deviation of return. These are measures of volatility or how much yield could vary around the expected or average yield. Sellers and buyers have totally different points of view in evaluating offers. A seller will look at a stock offer primarily in terms of that stock's market price and the total value of the offer. The buyer, on the other hand, should consider the risk involved in making the purchase and determine a price based on that risk.

As stated previously, value is based on expected results, not past performance. When evaluating future performance, consider whether the company will perform well in the future. When you judge the target's risk to be the same as your overall risk, the appropriate rate for discounting the candidate's cash flow stream is your cost of capital. The cost of capital, or minimum acceptable rate of return on investment, is based on the rate you might expect to earn by investing in other equally risky securities. Usually, the higher the risk, the higher the rate of return required.

Note that your company's use of its own cost of capital to discount the target company's projected cash flow is appropriate only when you can safely assume that the acquisition will not affect the riskiness of your own company. The specific riskiness of each target should be taken into account in setting the discount rate higher for more risky investments.

You can cope with risk two ways: You can make a downward adjustment to the expected future stream (earnings, cash flow, dividends, and so forth) to reflect the uncertainty. Or, you can use an increased discount rate in valuing the expected stream. You may use a combination of these methods.

Bierman and Smidt* argue that the theoretically correct way to handle risk is to adjust the future expectations stream to a "certainty-adjusted equivalent." Expectations are adjusted downward by some factor reflecting the possibility that they will not be achieved. Then the same cost of capital is applied to the valuation of all other investment choices. Cost of capital is the rate of return available in the marketplace on investments of comparable risk.

Another way to look at risk is to compare the return given to a risk-free investment with the expected return in the acquisition of the target company. The rate of return in excess of the risk-free rate is known as the risk premium. Thus the risk premium is the extra return you require because you are taking additional risks.

6.2 VALUATION TECHNIQUES

Several valuation techniques are commonly used in acquisitions. The following methods are reviewed in detail:

1. Discounted cash flow
2. Comparable company analysis
   —P/E ratio
   —Dividend capitalization

* Harold Bierman, Jr., and Seymour Smidt, *The Capital Budgeting Decision*, 4th edition. New York: Macmillan Company, 1975.

3. Market capitalization
4. Book value
5. Asset appraisal

DISCOUNTED CASH FLOW Discounted cash flow relates the present to the future. Valuing a corporate enterprise using this approach involves the following steps:

- Estimating the cash flow that may be realized from an investment in the target over time
- Setting the period of the future cash flow
- Discounting projected returns to a present value. This step requires selecting an interest rate to reflect the time value of money and then adjusting that number by an appropriate risk factor.
- Discounting the terminal value of the enterprise to the present.

The value of the company is the present worth of the cash flow, plus the present worth of the residual assets, less any remaining liabilities. The theoretical foundation of discounted cash flow analysis is constructed from three hypotheses:

1. Cash now is worth more than an equal amount of cash in the future.
2. Future cash flows, such as from business operations, are reasonably predictable.
3. The marginal cost of capital available to the business and its alternative returns on invested capital are similar and may be estimated.

The major difference between earnings capitalization and the discounted cash flow method is that after-tax earnings are discounted instead of cash flow. Cash flow is generally considered a purer number than earnings because earnings can change significantly, if based on different accounting conventions. "Cash flow," however, is neither cash nor flow; some analysts consider it working capital because it represents only net changes resulting from operations.

Cash flow may be defined as:

(Earnings before interest and taxes [EBIT] × (1 − income tax rate)

+ depreciation and other noncash adjustments to earnings

— capital expenditures
— cash for increase in net working capital

In developing the cash-flow schedule, the horizon date should be considered (this is the date beyond which cash flows associated with the acquisition are not specifically projected). Precisely how the residual value of the acquisition is established at this horizon date should also be examined at this time.

In working out cash-flow forecasts and determining what discount to apply to the projected returns, remember that a financial forecast is an attempt to describe future events in numerical terms. There are sophisticated techniques for testing the reliability of forecasts and showing how important each assumption is to the final outcome. Most important in reviewing a forecast is to critically analyze the relationship of the key figures, such as inventories to sales, receivables to sales, sales per dollar of capital, profit margins and rates of return on capital. Are these relationships realistic?

Buyers can work toward a time value of the target company by following the capital asset pricing model approach to the financial components of a company. These components are debt (K_i), equity (K_e), and preferred stock (K_{ps}). The equation below for K_A, the weighted average cost of capital, shows the relationships among these components.

$$K_A = W_i K_i (1 - t) + W_e K_e (lev) + W_{ps} K_{ps}$$

The weighted average cost of capital of a company, K_A, is determined through the relationships of the following variables. The weight of debt of the company is expressed as W_i, which is the weight of debt in the capital structure. K_i, the cost of debt capital, is determined through:

$$K_i = E (R)_{riskless} + [(market\ bond\ yields) - E(R)_{riskless}]\ \beta_i$$

If we define the market to be the market for fixed return securities, the beta coefficient (β_i) will approach the value of one and thereby simplify the above equation. The next variable, t, is equal to the tax rate of the acquirer.

W_e is the weight of *equity* in the capital structure. K_e (lev) is the leveraged cost of equity capital, and is expressed through:

$$K_e (lev) = K_e (unlev) + (K_e (unlev) - K_i (1 - t)]\frac{W_i}{W_e}$$

The unleveraged cost of equity capital is computed from:

$$K_e \text{ (unlev)} = E(R)_{riskless} + [R(\text{market portfolio}) - E(R)_{riskless}] \beta_e$$

W_{ps} is the weight of preferred stock in the capital structure. K_{ps} is the cost of preferred stock and is determined through:

$$K_{ps} = E(R)_{riskless} + [R(\text{similar preferred stock}) - E(R)_{riskless}] \beta_{ps}$$

β equals the measurement of risk for each capital source (β_i for debt, β_e for equity, and β_{ps} for preferred stock). β for debt and preferred stock is determined through:

$$\beta_i = \beta_{ps} = 1 \text{ (approximately)}$$

COMPARABLE COMPANY ANALYSIS

The comparable company approach is used to objectively determine proper capitalization rates by comparing the prospective seller to other companies in the same industry. The companies should have similar financial, operating, and marketing characteristics, as well as similar overall risks.

The strength of this method is that it draws on actual transactions between purchasers and sellers to approximate the definition of fair market value. Factors to be looked at include the following:

- Return on sales
- Return on assets
- Return on equity
- Price-to-earnings (P/E) ratio

Insurance companies, for instance, can be priced quite accurately on the basis of the number of dollars of insurance premiums of different types on the books, using actuarial tables and assumed earnings rates on invested reserves. The market price of the capital stock of the target company, or of the stocks of public companies in the same industry, is always a potent factor in arriving at overall valuation.

Return on sales, assets, and equity may be calculated easily. A comparative P/E analysis should follow. The closing prices on the average price for the year are divided by twelve-months earnings to arrive at the P/E ratio. A weighting factor usually is included. P/E ratios will be examined more closely later.

There are other financial areas that can be analyzed to compare the target company with others:

1. Percent of pretax profit to sales
2. Percent of gross profit to sales
3. Current ratio
4. Inventory turnover
5. Receivable turnover
6. Debt-to-equity ratio
7. Compounded annual sales and earnings growth
8. Potential earnings

When comparable companies are used, the P/E ratios and/or the dividends-to-price ratios of the companies are applied to the earnings and/or dividends of the target company. The comparable-companies technique is the one most frequently used by underwriters.

Even though two companies may appear to be comparable, significant differences can still exist in several accounting areas:

1. Inventory costing method
2. Depreciation methods
3. Amortization of intangibles
4. Allowances
5. Pension plan funding and accruals
6. Research and development expenses
7. Purchase and sales discounts
8. Bad debts

Differences can exist in nonaccounting areas as well:

1. Differences in product lines
2. Degree of horizontal and vertical integration
3. Geographic sales patterns
4. Amount of sales to governmental units
5. Capital structure and its leverage effect on earnings

How can you tell when two companies are comparable? Companies may be considered comparable if they react to changes in the economy in the same manner. A comparable company may sell to the same, or a similar market, even though it does not sell the same product. The following criteria should be considered when assessing comparability: number and size of retail outlets, sales or net income volume, product mix, and territory of operations.

Sales of comparable companies, especially listed or publicly owned companies, must be examined. The competitive position of the target company is of major importance, as is the state of the national economy. The primary purpose of a historical comparative study is to assess the effects of past events and current trends on future earnings and cash flows.

Two specific techniques most often used to carry out the comparable companies approach are P/E ratio and dividend capitalization.

COMPARABLE COMPANY ANALYSIS (P/E RATIO)

The P/E ratio is a multiplier applied to the after-tax earnings of the target company. The target company can be valued by analyzing the P/E ratios applicable to publicly traded companies considered to be reasonably comparable to the company being valued.

P/E is the total market value of the company divided by its after-tax earnings. Total market value is equal to the company's stock price multiplied by the total number of shares outstanding. P/E is an indication of the value the market places on the company's earnings. Table 6–1 is an example of a comparative P/E ratio analysis. Figures indicate stock prices divided by earnings per share. The weighting factors are used to place greater emphasis on current P/Es than on earlier P/Es. This produces a more realistic analysis because it focuses on current performance while at the same time taking a long-term outlook into account. When using this technique it is important to remember the following points:

1. Overall P/E levels fluctuate with changes in the market and the economy as a whole.
2. Current P/Es reflect only past earnings.
3. The quality of earnings can vary.
4. Future P/E estimates are only as valid as the earnings estimates themselves.
5. Seller's earnings may be overstated, resulting in an inflated valuation when applying a P/E that is considered an industry norm.

Although often useful in obtaining an accurate assessment of a company's value, P/E ratios can be easily misinterpreted for the follow-

TABLE 6–1
Price/Earnings Ratio Analysis ($000)

Company Name	Price/Earnings Ratio		
	1983	1984	1985
A	27	24	20
B	23	21	17
C	18	20	18
Total:	68	65	55
	÷ 3	÷ 3	÷ 3
Average P/E:	22.7	21.7	18.3

Year	(1) Average P/E Ratio	(2) Weighted Factor	(3) Weighted Average P/E Ratio
			(1) × (2)
1985	18.3	6	109.8
1984	21.7	3	65.1
1983	22.7	1	22.7
Total:		10	197.6
			÷ 10
Average P/E			19.8

(4) Average P/E Ratio	(5) Target Company's After-tax Earnings	(6) Target Company Valuation
		(5) × (6)
19.8	$646	$12,790.8

ing reasons: Remember that sellers tend to be unwilling to accept a price that represents a P/E ratio much below the market-determined P/E ratio of comparable companies. If the earnings used turn out to be inaccurate, or if there are no publicly traded companies that are truly comparable, the P/E ratio pricing conclusion may be distorted.

COMPARABLE
COMPANY
ANALYSIS
(DIVIDEND
CAPITALIZATION)

In order to look at dividend capitalization, it is necessary to first find comparable companies, just as was done for the P/E ratio. A typical dividend yield rate is then selected for them. That is, one rate is chosen that would be reasonably representative for all of the comparable companies.

The "dividend-paying capacity" of the target company is developed next. This factor may be higher or lower than that of the actual dividends paid, depending on whether the company is closely held or publicly owned. The dividend-paying capacity is a judgment of how much of the company's earnings can appropriately be devoted to paying dividends.

The final step is to divide the dividend-paying capacity by the typical dividend yield rate. In effect, the dividend yield rate is used as a capitalization rate, the result being another measure of the value of the assessed company.

Although there is no esoteric formula to determine the weight (if any) that should be assigned to the dividend capitalization analysis in developing the valuation judgment, most experts would agree that the price/earnings analysis should be given more weight than the dividend capitalization analysis.

Table 6–2 illustrates the dividend capitalization approach.

MARKET
CAPITALIZATION

The market value of a common stock generally sets a floor for the offering price. If the seller is a publicly traded company, it will be difficult to make the acquisition without offering a premium over the stock market price. The market price may or may not reflect the seller's base value, but as a practical matter, the market price significantly affects the seller's self-evaluation.

Stock prices in the open market may offer a basis for assessing the comparative worth of the acquiring corporation and the target corporation. The market value (which reflects factors such as prospects, stability, and risk) is used to determine an approximate exchange ratio. This is the ratio of shares that the buyer will offer to the target's shareholders for each of their shares. Many different exchange ratios may be established, using the following factors:

TABLE 6–2
Dividend Capitalization Analysis ($000)

Year	(1) Market Capitalization Comparable Co. A	B	(2) Dividends Paid Comparable Co. A	B	(3) Dividend Yield Comparable Co. A	B	(4) Weighting Factor Comparable Co. A	B
					(2) ÷ (1)			
1981	$10,000	$ 6,000	$1,000	$ 500	10.0%	8.3%	10%	5%
1982	11,000	8,000	1,200	700	10.9%	8.8%	20%	10%
1983	12,000	10,000	1,400	900	11.7%	9.0%	20%	15%
1984	13,000	12,000	1,600	1,000	12.3%	8.3%	25%	30%
1985	14,000	14,000	1,800	1,200	12.9%	8.6%	25%	40%
							100%	100%

Year	(5) Weighted Dividend Yield Rate Comparable Co. A	B	(6) Weighting Factor Comparable Co. A	B	(7) Weighted Dividend Yield Rate Comparable Co. A	B
	(3) × (4)	(3) × (4)			(5) × (6)	(5) × (6)
1981	1.0%	.4%				
1982	2.2%	.9%				
1983	2.3%	1.4%				
1984	3.1%	2.5%				
1985	3.2%	3.4%				
Total	11.8%	8.6%	60%	40%	7.1%	3.4%

Year	(8) Summary Comparable Co. Dividend Yield Rate	(9) Target Company Dividend Paying Capacity	(10) Target Company Valuation
	(7a) + (7b)		(9) ÷ (8)
1981		$ 700	
1982		900	
1983		1,100	
1984		1,250	
1985		1,450	
		5,400	
		÷ 5	
Total	10.5%	$1,080	$10,285.7

1. Historical earnings for the latest year
2. The average of historical earnings for the last five years, more than five years, or less than five years
3. Projected earnings for the ensuing year or several years
4. A combination of any of the three earnings figures described above

Proponents of the market capitalization approach to valuation argue that actual market values are set by the two parties acting in their own self-interests. Thus, the price embodies appraisals of presumed experts who are willing to support their opinions with cash. The prices at which sales take place are practical expressions of value instead of theoretical abstractions.

Detractors of the method point out that a market requires the existence of market price. Unfortunately, not all companies have their stock traded on the exchanges. Moreover, even among the listed companies' stock, there is a wide range of trading activity. Markets are especially thin for many securities traded in the over-the-counter market, where spreads between bid and asked prices can be very wide.

BOOK VALUE   The excess of assets over liabilities is called book value. (Book value is also known as shareholders' equity, net worth, or net assets.) There is no automatic relationship between book value and the market value of a company. Book values are important, but there is a tendency to distort their importance in valuations and price negotiations. Book value is not related to earnings history, cash flow, capacity, or potential, which are far more important in setting a price.

Book values are most useful in appraising companies whose assets are largely liquid and subject to fairly accurate accounting valuation. Book value's function is to serve as a measure of relative participation in the net worth of a company.

In most cases, book value approximates market value only by coincidence. The fair market value of underlying assets may be significant. If preferred stock is outstanding, the value of the preferred stock less preferred dividends payable usually is deducted from the total net worth to determine the net worth attributable to the common stock, which is then divided by the number of common shares outstanding to yield the book value per common share.

Some analysts exclude from book value intangible assets such as goodwill, as well as patents, organization expenses, and deferred charges. Others add to book value negative goodwill plus various reserve amounts judged to be segregations of surplus.

Book value is readily available. It has traditionally been understood by most businesspeople, accountants, lawyers, and by many laymen, who may be serving on juries where value is an issue. Furthermore, a careful test of the unadjusted balance sheet may indicate that there are factors on both sides that, taken together, result in a book value that by coincidence may be economic. One would be ill-advised to adopt the book net worth as the final value conclusion, however, without checking each item on the balance sheet carefully and without comparing book values shown on the balance sheet with those resulting from other valuation methods. As previously noted, differences in accounting policies can reduce the simplest book values to somewhat soft approximations.

ASSET APPRAISAL Valuation of a target company may also be based on an appraisal of the assets of that company. Early in structuring the deal, both parties should ascertain which assets will be transferred to you, the buyer. The following assets may or may not be transferred:

- Prepaid insurance
- Cash
- Marketable securities
- Accounts receivable
- Notes receivable

An appraisal of assets, particularly physical assets, is important to the buyer of an asset-rich business or a business with uncertain prospects. The most common approach to valuing intangibles is to discount future cash flows, either in the form of royalty savings afforded by ownership of the intangible (such as a patent), or the after-tax income associated with the intangible.

The asset-appraisal approach is particularly well-suited to businesses that derive value from underlying assets rather than from the prospect of an earnings stream. Valuation of assets is especially important in acquisitions to be accounted for by the purchase method where the difference, if any, between the purchase price and the value of the net assets acquired must be recorded as goodwill and amortized over a period not to exceed forty years. It is important to keep in mind that goodwill is not tax deductible, whereas an identifiable intangible can be deductible. Asset appraisal, however, is less suitable in cases where future earnings from the target, rather than appreciation in asset values, are the acquiror's main goal.

6.3 GENERAL ANALYSIS

We have described and examined a number of valuation methods. In each case, adequate preparation was seen as the major prerequisite to a successful acquisition.

You want to know if the price your company sets for an acquisition is too high or too low. Prepare yourself thoroughly, follow the four principles below, and you will address the issue of acquisition analysis as an intelligent professional.

1. Establish a valuation range.
2. Do not dilute earnings over the long term.
3. Incorporate the alternative investment principle into your analysis.
4. Test your assumptions with the payback analysis.

One way to establish price negotiation parameters is to specify a range (maximum/minimum) of values.

In most transactions and particularly in exchanges of capital stock, most successful acquirers endeavor not to dilute their earnings per share (EPS) after an acquisition or merger. This computation may be based, when practical, on prospective rather than historical earnings. It would be nice if earnings-per-share went up, but that is not necessary. A company can increase EPS by increasing leverage as long as the marginal return on investment is greater than the interest rate on the new debt. In any case, because reported EPS continues to be of great interest to the financial community and has a strong impact on the value of your own stock, a complete acquisition analysis should include a comparison of projected EPS both with and without the acquisition.

One may consider increasing EPS as an acquisition test. However, the effect of an acquisition on EPS of the acquiring company is dangerous when used as the sole approach to acquisition decision making. It works only in an ideal situation, as described below:

1. The target company has a well-balanced, high quality capital structure, and the growth rate in EPS is due entirely to investing the earnings in the company with a constant dividend payout ratio.
2. The buyer is in a similar financial condition, and the acquisition is financed so that afterwards the surviving entity has a balanced capital structure.

3. The risk of the target is the same as that of the buyer; or, if a difference in risk exists, there is a corresponding difference in capital structures.

In such a situation, the acquisition might be justified if it resulted in equaling or improving future EPS. However, consider factors that could affect the future combined growth rate in EPS from an acquisition, including these:

- The method of financing
- Growth in EPS due to an increase in rate of return or other transitory way in which EPS increase

The alternative investment principle should also be considered. This principle states that an investment in an acquisition must have an anticipated return greater than the return readily available from relatively risk-free alternative investments. These alternatives include treasury bills, certificates of deposits, government obligations, or high-grade corporate bonds. This principle is incorporated in the discounted cash-flow technique, discussed earlier.

An adjunct of the measurement of future earnings is the question of how long it will take for you to get back your investment from the target company. This measurement is known as payback analysis, and is the method most often used by industry to rank capital investment proposals. As a measure of risk, payback analysis is very useful. It is easy to see that the faster your initial capital outlay is recovered, the less time your capital is at risk.

Payback does not measure profitability, however. A payback evaluation ignores all of the cash flows expected after the payback period; post-recovery cash flows can be of vital importance to a project's profitability. Another major objection to payback is that it fails to consider the time value of money.

6.4 OTHER ISSUES

There are several other critical issues to consider in acquisitions, the details of which are beyond the scope of this book.

Structuring the transaction requires the assistance of financial, tax, and legal experts. For pricing purposes, you must know if you will be buying stock or selected assets and liabilities of the prospect, and whether you intend to pay with stock, notes, cash, or some combination thereof. You should have a general understanding of how transactions can be structured, when each structure is applicable, the advantages and disadvantages of each, and their current status in light of any recent accounting, tax, regulatory, or legislative changes.

The tax implications of a chosen structure are often the primary reason for its selection, and such implications must be examined from the standpoint both of the buyer and the seller. Being advised by experts who are fully knowledgeable of the latest tax laws is a must. Items such as tax recapture and the transferability of tax loss carryforwards can make or break a deal. You should take an aggressive stance in structuring a transaction by deciding what type of structure you want and then getting your financial advisors to figure out how to do it. Any offer you develop should be reviewed by a tax advisor to determine the tax implications and whether the transaction and offer could be structured in another, more advantageous way.

The structure of a transaction could produce a situation where different prices could be offered for the same company, depending on the structure, and where the transaction and offer could be structured in another way that would better meet the needs of both buyer and seller.

- A cash purchase could be higher than that proposed in a pooling with an exchange of securities because the purchaser would recover part of the price paid through reductions in federal income taxes resulting from a stepped-up tax basis of assets acquired. Also, a seller generally would require a higher price in a cash deal than in an exchange of securities because of immediate tax consequences.

- A company in an industry similar to that of the prospective seller might be willing to pay a top price because of the opportunity to integrate operations and increase sales and profits through the use of combined manufacturing and marketing facilities. Duplicate facilities may be eliminated in such a deal with resultant savings.

- An offer made solely for the purpose of putting funds to work without any intention of exercising influence on the management of the company would ordinarily be conservative, as an investor would expect the return on such an investment to be better than an investment in blue chip stocks or mutual funds.

Finally, consider the legal aspects of the purchase agreement. Be sure that you and your legal representatives follow SEC and any applicable regulatory rules, and make sure your financial advisor is aware of current developments in local and federal tax legislation.

Integration: The
Critical Component

7

7.1 INTRODUCTION

Before looking at integration—and finding out why it is the key component of a successful merger—here is a brief survey of the problems facing you, the would-be merger maker.

As we've noted before, most business mergers seem headed for failure. A key indicator of the degree to which mergers have failed is the fact that over a third of recent acquisitions have been followed by subsequent divestitures (which might be likened to corporate divorces).

Why such a horrendous track record? There are numerous reasons. A large company quite often smothers a small partner. It imposes its bureaucratic layers over those already in place. It stifles innovation and literally destroys whatever entrepreneurial resources the small company may have had. And in doing so, it destroys jobs as well.

On the other hand, when large companies merge it is most often the inability to combine bureaucracies that spells stagnation. If both bureaucracies survive, the giant's doom is assured.

Personnel problems are common and potentially disastrous. Firings often follow a takeover. Many key employees often leave. And some who stay give up and stop performing.

The unacceptably high failure rate is due in large measure to lack of planning. The would-be parent overestimates what the acquisition

107

can bring, and overestimates as well its own ability to manage the new company.

A Touche Ross survey on the effects of mergers and acquisitions on American business has identified problems likely to stand in the way of a successful merger. In that survey, 99 percent of respondents cited integration as the toughest hurdle to overcome (two thirds called it a "major problem." As one director put it: "It is very difficult to change the customs of a company. You have to change their accounting and control procedures, their policy manuals, their pension plan, their vacation policy. You have to accommodate two different management styles." A few corporations have been able to cope with this, but more often the dominant company makes a fetish of forcing the incoming group into its own pattern.

Time and time again, top executives identify integration as the key obstacle to—or critical component of—mergers and acquisitions. This chapter introduces common problems associated with integration and describes the integration process, using a three-phase approach that begins with a review of corporate goals and ends with standardization, control, and monitoring procedures that optimize the chances for a successful integration.

7.2 COMMON INTEGRATION PROBLEMS

Two types of problems are associated with integration. First, there are general problems, such as attitude. Should the proposed merger be taking place at all? And there are specific problems more likely to be associated with factors such as differences in management styles, and so forth. Problems that result from human resource considerations are common as well and are covered in the next section.

The motives of the parent corporation should be closely examined. You must have valid, rational reasons to acquire another company. Bigness alone isn't enough. Nor is fear that lack of growth will lead to destruction. Haphazard growth does not necessarily spell success, and momentum or enthusiasm are more easily dampened than stimulated. The reasons are sometimes selfish as well, such as wanting to be CEO of a large organization.

You should closely question your motives or assumptions about the new partner. Whereas you may find it relatively easy to convince, cajole, or coerce a small company's president to bless the merger, it is altogether different to expect everyone else to fall in line. Any organization that believes it can "manage" its acquisition into shape may be in for a rude awakening.

Combining companies means significant changes for all those involved. Successful integration calls for the management of those changes. If the necessary changes are not identified before the merger takes effect, or if the human resources needed to implement them are unavailable, the combination process will not go well. Management skills (and time) required to achieve the joint management task are often underestimated. The acquisition of a small company cannot necessarily be construed as requiring little management effort.

Because extra managerial skills are needed to handle the transition, you must assess the competence of the subsidiary's management *before* the merger takes place. Every effort must be made to preserve a capable management team and to identify potential conflicts before they become critical.

Two different approaches to mergers have been described as "strategic" and "opportunistic" mergers. Whereas the first category is characterized by careful planning (treating acquisitions as part of overall corporate strategy), the "opportunistic" merger is one in which the merger makers are reacting to opportunity. The planning approach is more likely to succeed, particularly if a top executive has been given the exclusive job to develop and implement a corporate acquisition program. One goal of such a program is to create *synergy*—that appealing phenomenon whereby the whole turns out to be greater than the sum of its parts.

Although synergy doesn't always live up to expectations, certain conditions can enhance your opportunity to make it pay off. This is true in the case of financial mergers, where the increased availability of capital improves your chances to do business. It is also true in the case of mergers that can eliminate duplicate marketing, financial, or organizational functions. Other factors that can contribute to synergy, though not as often, include shared technology or economies of scale (that produce better deals from suppliers).

Another common problem is the result of a mismatch between parent and subsidiary. Sometimes a large company simply stifles its small acquisition. In other instances, the small company looks to the parent as a bottomless source of capital, technology, management, and the like. Large parent corporate staffs inevitably make themselves felt at the subsidiary, and any resistance is interpreted as insubordination.

7.3 HUMAN RESOURCE PROBLEMS

Of all the problems likely to arise during mergers and acquisitions, those that involve human resources are the most pervasive and the most difficult to solve.

The fact that mergers often come as a surprise introduces uncertainty, mistrust, and discontentment among the employees of the company about to be taken over. Problems such as these are hard to overcome. Literally dozens of questions must be answered. How and where will people fit in the new organization? Here again, you must *manage change*.

You must lay the groundwork *before* the merger takes place. Will available skills meet anticipated needs? Are differences in management style likely to cause problems? Consultants may be called in to provide some of the answers. Special counseling techniques can help executives in charge of the transition, once the decision to merge has been made. It is especially important to avoid the common (and destructive) "we/ they" syndrome.

Attitude problems are often traced to a perceived loss of autonomy on the part of the acquired company's management. Inadequate, incomplete, or inaccurate exchanges of information between parent and subsidiary are another source of trouble (and can bring about poor decisions). Communication paths must be direct. Reportability must be clearly established.

The loss of management talent can make integration difficult. This is reflected in the postmerger track record of American business: fewer than 60 percent of an acquired company's top management are likely to stay on. Most executives who leave do so within a year or two, and many of these pirate key second-line managers. Coming at a time when the combined company has not had a chance to develop management backup, these defections can be very serious.

Although it would be naive to think that problems associated with human resources can be eliminated, you can take steps to lessen their impact. As noted above, most executives leave because they feel that the parent organization is interfering. Surveys indicate that parent companies that allow their subsidiaries to retain greater autonomy keep a higher percentage of their managers. And although it is best to decide quickly who stays, who goes, and on what terms, you should not make sudden policy changes, especially if they affect salaries and benefits, or involve relocations and reorganizations. Give employees the opportunity to adapt to their new environment.

You must evaluate the organizational climate of the company you are about to acquire—its efficiency, the likelihood that it will "fit in" the new organization. Are its people hard working? Are they team players? Where are conflicts most likely to arise? A department-by-department comparison between parent and subsidiary can identify potential trouble spots.

In brief summary, the preacquisition process is characterized by a careful assessment of management and other human resources available within the target company. It is essential that the skills required to manage integration are available. At the postdecision stage, integration shifts into high gear, and the emphasis turns to motivation. Goals must be unified, and management of change becomes the primary challenge. You must answer some important questions: Who will manage the subsidiary? Who will coordinate operations with the parent company? Where are conflicts likely to arise? (And if conflicts arise, how can they be resolved?)

7.4 THE INTEGRATION PROCESS

This section introduces a phased approach to the integration process, as shown in Figure 7–1. Before the process can begin, you should know the degree of integration that is going to be expected. If the corporate goal is growth within an industry segment, a tightly integrated division should be planned. However, if conglomerate growth is desired, subsidiaries must remain highly autonomous. Note that autonomy (freedom in managing day-to-day operations) does not imply lack of budgetary control, or uncoordinated corporate goals and strategies.

Preacquisition research and analysis is the process used to prepare for integration. As shown in Figure 7–2, this task is undertaken by the board of directors and top management of the parent company. The key elements of this essential prelude to integration are a review of corporate goals, and an assessment of resources (financial and human) required to pursue those goals.

As prospects indicate a greater likelihood that a merger or acquisition is about to take place, your next preacquisition activity is to determine the type of joint organization that will be created. What will its management style be like? What are its priorities? How autonomous will its subsidiaries be?

These decisions have far-reaching effects. Candor is essential at this stage of the process. There must be fundamental reasons for wanting to buy a company. In a 1982 *Forbes* interview, Peter Drucker quotes

Figure 7–1. The Integration Process

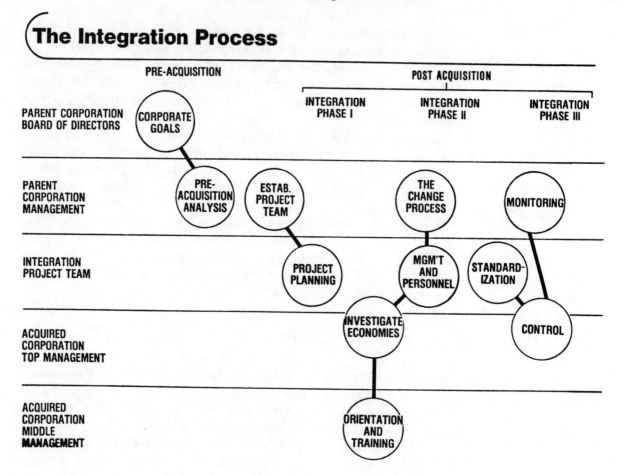

The Integration Process

Figure 7–2. Preacquisition activities

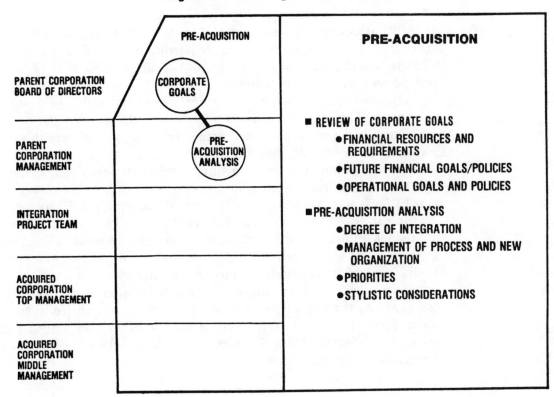

an early associate who questioned Drucker's interest in the balance sheet of a takeover candidate: "You are starting with the financial figures. That is wrong. One ends with them. You are talking of a marriage: one doesn't marry a girl without a dowry, but one first investigates her ancestors. First comes the ancestry. Then comes the girl. Finally, the dowry. The only thing that's negotiable is the dowry."

Thus, you should not consummate a deal simply because the price seems right. A "good" investment suggests that there's a market for what you're about to buy. As a rule, a smart company will make an acquisition if it feels it can gain access to a market or technology, or if it believes it can turn a business around and improve it drastically.

In the *Forbes* interview cited above, Mr. Drucker uses the example of Premier Industrial's acquisition record. Premier's approach is to study a business for six months to a year, and then to ask itself how that business might be drastically improved. Premier approaches the company's owner with its plan, suggesting that it be tried at no risk to the company. At the end of the trial, if both companies still feel it makes sense, Premier makes an offer—by letting the other side suggest a fair price and improving on it. Premier has succeeded 19 out of 20 times, a remarkable record.

PHASE I: INITIATING INTEGRATION

Once the groundwork has been laid and the preacquisition research and analysis is completed, you can begin the first phase of integration. As shown in Figure 7–3, Phase I consists of two principal steps: establishing the project team and project planning.

Both companies must participate in the selection of team members. Members should be thoroughly familiar with corporate goals and with operations in both companies. It is also important that those selected be given the time and resources to carry out their assignments. Liaison with the acquiring company must be close and straightforward.

As the team begins project planning, it first identifies and prioritizes the issues that are most critical to achieving integration. If implementation of the parent company's plan calls for changes, make them early—when management and employees expect them. However, it is wise to hold off on controversial demands or changes (such as relocations or reorganizations).

Replacing managers who report to the new subsidiary after acquisition has taken place is an especially sensitive task. You should give the CEO of the acquired company a say in the selection of a new management team. Clearly assign responsibilities for the timely implementation of a feasible and mutually agreeable work plan. And establish direct

Figure 7–3. Phase I

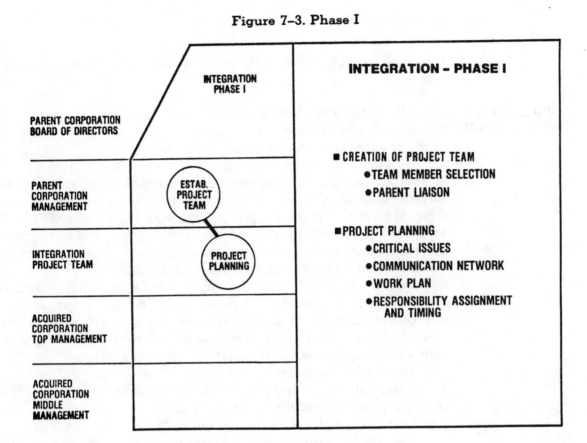

communication channels—both within the subsidiary and across companies.

IMPLEMENTING CHANGE

Phase II of the integration process involves the parent company's top management and the integration team. It also requires the participation of the acquired company's top and middle management.

As shown in Figure 7–4, Phase II includes four activities. First comes the investigation of opportunities for realizing economies across various functions. The next step involves training the human resources required to carry out the integration process. Here the emphasis is on team building and information transfer. The third step consists of management and personnel considerations. You must define and establish communication channels and reporting relationships. And you must be sure that your work force will fulfill its role—that both numbers and skills will be adequate. The final activity in Phase II is to manage change. You must resolve all key personnel issues. As previously noted, this is a difficult and important task. On the one hand, you must pursue agreed-to goals, but you must be careful not to trample egos.

Monitoring the integration process, the third and final phase of the integration process, is shown in Figure 7–5. It requires the participation of the parent company's management, the top management of the target company, and the integration project team.

You should begin Phase III by standardizing key processes within the subsidiary. The integration team must first establish clear management reporting procedures. Accounting methods, inventory controls, audit procedures, and personnel policies (including evaluation and compensation) are also implemented in this step.

In the second step, you must establish budgetary and operational controls. Marketing and sales policies should also be coordinated to ensure that they mesh with overall corporate goals.

The final step in Phase III monitors earlier activities to ensure that integration is proceeding on a healthy path. You must determine whether or not plan tasks are being carried out on schedule, you must compare financial performance against objectives, and you should see how well you've been able to hang on to key personnel.

In summary, integration is the critical element, the factor that either makes or breaks a merger or acquisition. The primary requirements of integration include careful planning and analysis, especially at the preacquisition stage. Identify and address problems before they become critical. Find the human resources required to manage the transition. And monitor performance against a formal integration plan.

As stated at the start of this book, a structured program and hard

Figure 7-4. Phase II

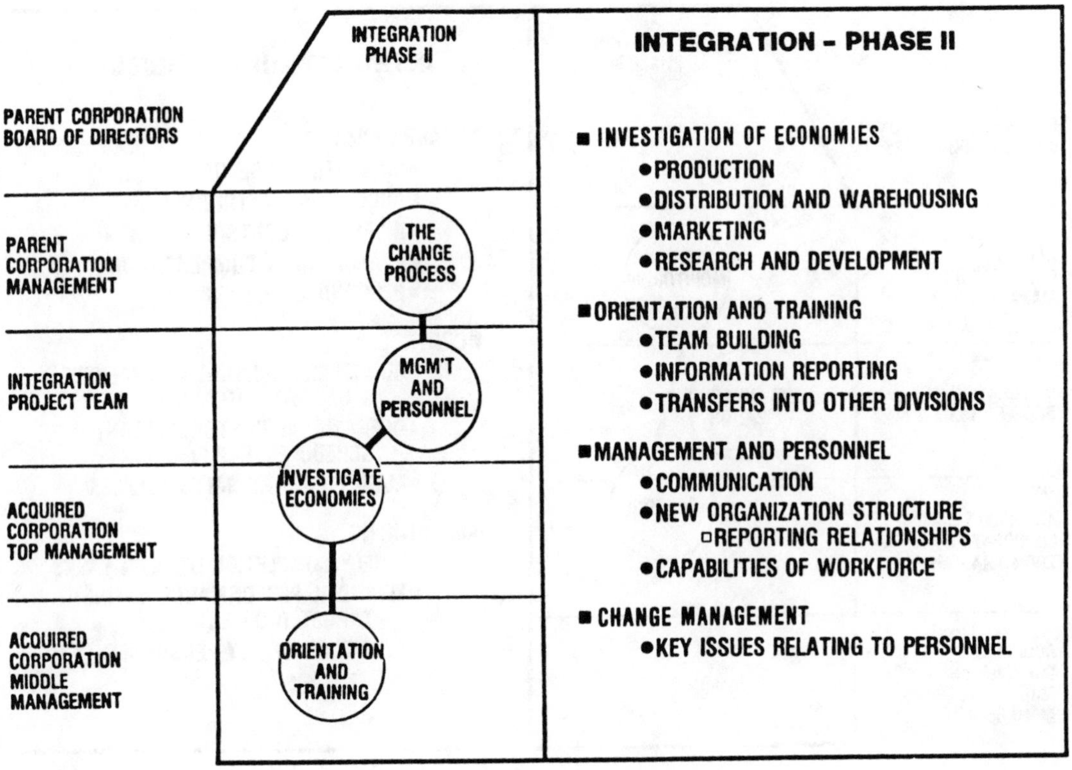

INTEGRATION PHASE II

PARENT CORPORATION BOARD OF DIRECTORS

PARENT CORPORATION MANAGEMENT

INTEGRATION PROJECT TEAM

ACQUIRED CORPORATION TOP MANAGEMENT

ACQUIRED CORPORATION MIDDLE MANAGEMENT

THE CHANGE PROCESS

MGM'T AND PERSONNEL

INVESTIGATE ECONOMIES

ORIENTATION AND TRAINING

INTEGRATION – PHASE II

■ INVESTIGATION OF ECONOMIES
  ● PRODUCTION
  ● DISTRIBUTION AND WAREHOUSING
  ● MARKETING
  ● RESEARCH AND DEVELOPMENT

■ ORIENTATION AND TRAINING
  ● TEAM BUILDING
  ● INFORMATION REPORTING
  ● TRANSFERS INTO OTHER DIVISIONS

■ MANAGEMENT AND PERSONNEL
  ● COMMUNICATION
  ● NEW ORGANIZATION STRUCTURE
    □ REPORTING RELATIONSHIPS
  ● CAPABILITIES OF WORKFORCE

■ CHANGE MANAGEMENT
  ● KEY ISSUES RELATING TO PERSONNEL

117

Figure 7-5. Phase III

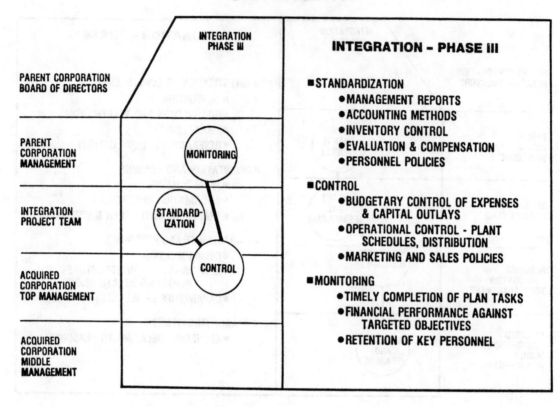

INTEGRATION PHASE III

PARENT CORPORATION BOARD OF DIRECTORS

PARENT CORPORATION MANAGEMENT

MONITORING

INTEGRATION PROJECT TEAM

STANDARD-IZATION

ACQUIRED CORPORATION TOP MANAGEMENT

CONTROL

ACQUIRED CORPORATION MIDDLE MANAGEMENT

INTEGRATION – PHASE III

■ STANDARDIZATION
- MANAGEMENT REPORTS
- ACCOUNTING METHODS
- INVENTORY CONTROL
- EVALUATION & COMPENSATION
- PERSONNEL POLICIES

■ CONTROL
- BUDGETARY CONTROL OF EXPENSES & CAPITAL OUTLAYS
- OPERATIONAL CONTROL - PLANT SCHEDULES, DISTRIBUTION
- MARKETING AND SALES POLICIES

■ MONITORING
- TIMELY COMPLETION OF PLAN TASKS
- FINANCIAL PERFORMANCE AGAINST TARGETED OBJECTIVES
- RETENTION OF KEY PERSONNEL

118

work are your best hope for a successful deal. We've seen corporate mergers taking place at an accelerated pace in recent years. In 1984, for instance, the Gulf-Socal and Getty-Texaco mergers alone accounted for over $23 billion in cash. The biggest winners in such deals are often speculators. With external forces at work, it is little wonder that so many corporate marriages wind up on the rocks. It has become ever more important that you establish a good fit between your company and a candidate for merger or acquisition. The combined company must capitalize on the strength of its parts, and the deal must support your company's growth plan.

Throughout this book, the emphasis has been to create a framework in which intuition can combine with hard work, analysis, and vigilance to produce a successful merger or acquisition.

Index